5 WORSHIP TEAM KILLERS

TRAVIS AGNEW

5 WORSHIP TEAM KILLERS

Copyright © 2017 by Travis Agnew
Tag Publishing
All rights reserved.
Printed in the United States of America

ISBN-13: 978-1542359665
ISBN-10: 154235966X

Scripture quotations are from The Holy Bible, English Standard Version © 2001 by Crossway Bibles, a publishing ministry of Good News Publishers. Used by permission. All rights reserved.

All rights reserved. No part of this publication may be reproduced, stored, in a retrieval system, or transmitted in any form or by any means - electronic, mechanical, photocopy, recording, or any other - except for brief quotations in printed reviews, without the prior permission of the publisher.

To the members of North Side Worship,

One of the highest privileges of my life
was pointing people to Jesus right alongside you.

CONTENTS

INTRO	9
1: PRIDE	27
2: INCONSISTENCY	45
3: INABILITY	63
4: DETACHMENT	83
5: DIVISION	103
CONCLUSION	123

*"**Great** is the LORD, and **greatly** to be praised, and his **greatness** is unsearchable"* (Psalm 145:3).

INTRODUCTION

"But the hour is coming, and is now here, when the true worshipers will worship the Father in spirit and truth, for the Father is seeking such people to worship him" (John 4:23).

Worship was never meant to be about me.

Yet that truth has not stopped me from attempting to make it about me every single day of my life. From the very beginning, the human heart has made worship about personal desires rather than selfless offerings. Unfortunately, those who serve in worship ministries have acquired a front row seat to the whole debacle. While it is easy to denounce casual worship attenders for their critical spirits when the service doesn't appease their preferential palates, deep down the same sin lingers in me. I want to make everything – even the worship of Jesus – all about me.

When I rate worship services based upon the degree of my personal satisfaction regarding aesthetic tastes, musical preferences, and sermon predispositions, I have reduced worship to idolatry and made the idol none other than myself. Sitting haughtily upon the judges' panel, I believe that those leading are only able to pass on to the next level of competition if they pass my esteemed appraisal. Instead of using biblical qualifications, I base everything upon personalized expectations. The worship service is labeled good only if I acquired a sufficient amount of warm and fuzzies.

When did worship ever become about what we got out of it?

Instead of keeping worship Godward, we have turned it inward. It's frightening to think of how many worship services people have attended and yet never stirred their affections towards Jesus in those moments. It's even more terrifying to think about how long people can serve on a worship team without ever actually intentionally directing people's affections toward Jesus.

Worshipers must realize that worship is not about them. Worship leaders must realize that worship is not about them. Those who lead others towards Jesus have to keep that focus as their goal and never get sidelined by lesser pursuits.

I can't lead you somewhere if I don't know the way.

While that admission seems like an obvious statement, the reality of such a concept can be tragically forgotten in our churches. In worship, the goal is to respond to God's revelation by ascribing to the LORD the glory that is due his name (1 Chr 16:29) by sacrificial offerings of praise and thanksgiving (Heb 13:15). The gathering of God's people (Ps 50:5; 1 Cor 14:26) is a needed pause from the routine in order to proclaim the goodness of our God corporately (Ps 34:3; 40:9; 100:4-5; 149:1). As a worship leader, if I'm not aligned with that direction, how could I ever expect the congregation to arrive there?

It's unfeasible that I could lead worship if I'm not a worshiper myself, and it's just as difficult to lead worship with those who aren't worshipers themselves. From the one in charge to every support position on the worship team, we cannot lead people to a place we are not going ourselves. The role of pointing others to worship the living God should be a terrifying position in which to serve. If done poorly, we could stand in the way of others seeing Jesus clearly. Do we understand the critical nature of our worship teams?

Too often, our church platforms elevate people whose desire is set on receiving praise more than it is about giving praise.

Through selfish motives, hidden agendas, and misplaced priorities, a poorly discipled worship team can dramatically alter a church's worship trajectory. I am confident of this possibility because I know my own heart. I understand this hazard because I have endured through many difficult conversations regarding the complexities of worship. I believe this because I have heard more church worship horror stories than I care to count. In my times as a worshiper and a worship leader, I have seen havoc break out when a congregation, team, or individual sets their sights on themselves rather than God.

Whether you are a worshiper or worship leader, the danger is consequential. Regardless of your ministry's worship style, no one receives immunity from this disease. It does not matter what your role is on the worship team, your soul needs constant and comprehensive evaluations. I believe your ministry is in danger because mine has been and continues to be. In reality, many of the most damaging sins have not always been sins of commission but sins of omission.

Unintentional & Dangerously Content

I never set out to become a worship pastor, but I did feel called to serve as a pastor. So when our pastoral staff decided to restart our church's focus with a blank page, I honestly had no idea where any of us would land regarding positions. If I still had a job on staff, I wasn't sure what that job would be.

We had grown overwhelmed with the busyness of the church calendar and were honestly unsure concerning the effectiveness of our activity. We were busy with good things but we were not confident if our efforts could classify as the best things we could have been doing. Somewhere in the process, we decided to simplify all that we did around equipping our people to live lifestyles of worship, discipleship, and mission. At that retreat, the responsibility of all our worship services was handed to me.

I became the worship pastor – on paper.

It wasn't till many months later that I became the worship pastor in reality though. In the transitioning months, I was charged with overseeing all of the worship elements from the cradle to the grave. I had a lot to learn. There were numerous things going well. I found myself celebrating so many parts of what was going on through the worship environments of our church.

I also realized that some challenges were looming ahead. Some of them were easy fixes and some of them were going to be longer ordeals to navigate through. Overwhelmed with the amount of potential present in our church, I struggled to discern which ministry hills needed to be crossed and which ones I would need to die upon.

If It Ain't Broke…

One of my greatest challenges was dealing with perception versus reality. So much of what I saw was quality. If it ain't broke, don't fix it, right? That type of mentality has two issues though:

1. It might not be broken, but it may be in the process of breaking.
2. It might not be broken, but it may not be currently utilized at full potential.

The group of volunteer worship leaders I inherited was stellar. Not only were they remarkably gifted, but they were extremely humble and godly. Any worship pastor would have coveted my position regarding the quality of people whom I had leading alongside me.

My greatest temptation was leaving them just the way they were.

The team was so outstanding, what could I show them? Not only was I younger than everyone on the team, but I felt that I was the least qualified and the least talented of the entire group. My intention was to keep things just as they were and not disrupt something so robust.

There was only one problem: I was called to be a pastor.

Like I stated earlier, I was never passionate about becoming a worship pastor. I don't say that because I devalue the position or the tasks associated with it. That could not be further from the truth.

I am extremely passionate about worship. I love the musical side of things. I cherish the gathering of the entire church body. While that aspect is an important part of a church, it is a minimal portion within the life of a church.

Think about it: how many minutes a week are we the church? Many people will answer it incorrectly by summarizing that the church is an hour-long service on a Sunday morning. If you read the Bible, you will realize that we are not called to *go* to church – we *are* the church.

There are 10,080 minutes in a week which means we are called to be the church every single one of those minutes. We are called to encourage others, serve those in need, reach out to the lost, study God's Word together, disciple the next generations, pray together, and so many other blessed activities. With so much to be done, we have no choice but to be the church for 10,080 minutes a week.

How much is music a part of the church? Anywhere from 15-30 minutes a week. If you do the math, that means that .1% of your church's activities is music, and yet in many places, the music is what gets the most attention – whether positive or negative.

Many churches allow 100% of their identity to be determined by .1% of their activity.

It is a tragic distraction to keep our eyes off of all that the church is supposed to be. Worship is a very big thing, but the church is so much more than just the musical selections shared within a few minutes each week. Not only is worship more than music but also pastoring is more involved than just leading certain programs within the timeframe of a church's weekly calendar.

Every pastor needs to wrestle with this thought because while we all agree that worship is an integral part of the church, we must acknowledge that the role of the worship pastor is not listed in the job descriptions contained within the New Testament. Pastoring is listed but not worship pastoring (as well as many other jobs on staff). That doesn't mean that we shouldn't have those positions, but we need to make sure that those positions are filled by people who are carrying out biblical expectations of church leadership.

Before I was asked by our elders to serve as a worship pastor, I was called by God to serve as a pastor. As a pastor, I am confident of certain job descriptions. I am called to:

1. *Equip* the saints for the work of the ministry (Eph 4:12)
2. *Shepherd* the flock among me (1 Pet 5:2)
3. *Feed* with knowledge and understanding (Jer 3:15)
4. *Provide* order for the church body (Titus 1:5)
5. *Watch* over the congregation's souls (Heb 13:17)
6. *Bear* the weight of teaching (James 3:1)
7. *Maintain* sound doctrine (Titus 2:1)
8. And so much more.

Develop Services or Disciples?

I had to choose if I was going to spend my time developing services or developing disciples.

At some point, I decided to go with the latter. I realized that if this great group of disciples could turn into a great group of disciple-makers, the church would change. I wanted to challenge, equip, and disciple our worship leaders.

Even while I didn't know all of the implications, I at least realized the need. I knew I needed to go somewhere even though I didn't know "where" that was (Heb 11:8). As I tried to talk myself out from leading in this direction, I struggled concerning my own inabilities. If I jump ahead of the pack and tell others to follow me, the scrutiny would increase. The potential of tension could escalate. Will I ever be able to tell them to imitate me as I imitate Christ (1 Cor 11:1)? With a false sense of humility, I considered not meddling in any attempts to further disciple this group.

Unfortunately, I couldn't rest there. Preparing to lead worship one Sunday morning, I had this nagging thought that would not leave my mind:

If I don't lead these people where they need to go, it's not humility –it's negligence.

For the worshipers in our congregation and the worship team under my leadership, my negligence would affect more than just me. I repented from my unintentionally and started trying to do what I felt the Bible was calling me to do. The following years would reveal many realities:

1. People want to be led.
2. People need to desire the destination in order to endure the journey.
3. Those leading will grow just as much as those following.
4. God will do extraordinary acts with our ordinary attempts.

My lack of intentionality up to this point was convicting. I confessed to the team that I had not been faithful to God's charge on my life, and I understood things had to change. We were going to grow as a group. We were going to mature as individuals. We were going to raise the bar in every way possible.

The Firing

So, what did I do? I fired the entire worship team. I must confess to you that none of them were paid or are currently paid. I just wanted us to renew the vows so to speak.

I called a worship team meeting and told them of my commitment to disciple them. We discussed what it would take for the individuals and for the team to develop. I then explained that within two months of that meeting, all existing members would be fired. The worship team as we knew it would cease to exist.

In a sea of confused glances, I passed around a document that I wanted them to pray through. The document contained the biblical reasoning for the worship team's new expectations. In it, I highlighted five potential worship team killers and the biblical response to combat each of them. At the back of the document was a thorough application that dealt more with doctrinal theology and personal testimony than vocal harmony and music theory. It was lovingly referred to by team members as the "theology exam."

I told them that I would be willing to lead worship all by my lonesome when the deadline had passed, but I would much rather be surrounded by a group of disciples who were committed to leading worship biblically. If they wanted to join this team, they would need to study, pray, and reapply.

Two months later, I had a completely different worship team:

1. Some people decided not to come back.
2. Some people decided to join us.
3. Some people decided to return with an increased level of dedication.

It was a different team completely. I didn't think that something so great could actually get better, but it did. Year after year, this group of disciples took their roles seriously. We simply didn't have issues. There was no diva demanding a solo. There was no bickering that turned practice into rehearsals for Armageddon. These people realized that they were family and took their role in the Body of Christ very solemnly.

The 5 Things

In my experience serving on worship teams throughout my life and in my time consulting with other worship ministries, it seemed to me that all of the issues that groups were facing could be compressed to five critical issues. It didn't matter if it was a choir or a band, contemporary or traditional, church plant or established church, these five issues came up repeatedly. It might have been a different flavor depending upon the context, but these issues seemed to rear their ugly head in every worship ministry I encountered.

While we will unpack these topics in the remainder of this book, let me at least expose you to the five worship team killers:

1. **Pride** - Gifted people can often turn into entitled people. If not careful, we can begin to believe the lie that we made our gifts rather than received our gifts (1 Cor 4:7). This pride assassin is so dangerous because God proactively opposes prideful worship teams (James 4:6). If we honestly grasp our conditions in light of the holiness of God, pride should be found killed rather than it be found killing us.

2. **Inconsistency** - Our stage portrayal should not be a soul betrayal. Those who dwell with the LORD must possess a sense of integrity (Ps 15:1-2). The LORD despises worship from a talented mouth that cannot be backed with a sincere heart (Isa 29:13). Our public worship should never exceed our private devotion. Worship should be an overflow from our hearts (Matt 12:34), and yet we must never desire our holiness to be noticed by others which provides a lesser reward (Matt 6:5-6) and devalues why we strive for integrity.

3. **Inability** - We tend to tolerate mediocre offerings because it's "only" church. Worship teams are supposed to lead in an excellent manner (Ps 33:3). Our God is great and so our offerings should come from us in such a way that it acknowledges the degree of his greatness (2 Sam 24:24). On the other extreme, leading with excellence in order to be praised is just as dangerous. Flashy performance can distract from authentic worship (Matt 6:1).

4. **Detachment** - Even if your church doesn't have a green room for the worship team to prepare, many churches have a green room mentality. The worship team functions physically on the stage but relationally on a separate island from the rest of the church. Platform ministry can never replace relational ministry. Sheep need shepherds (Matt 9:36). No matter how quality your presentation is, you will have minimal impact if you have minimal influence (Gal 6:2).

5. **Division** - Not only can a worship team detach from the congregation, they can distance themselves from one another. Artistic people can tend to suffer from beta fish syndrome – they only work well when kept away from others. We must fight against selfish isolation and divisive bickering. Worship teams lead as a part of the Body of Christ (1 Cor 12:27), and we must learn how to put others' desires above our own (Phil 2:3-4). Disagreements will happen, but is your team willing to address them biblically? It makes no sense to worship our Father while we tear down his children (1 John 4:19-20).

For the next year or so, we unpacked those five worship team killers as a group in our local church. Before weekly worship practice began, we spent time talking about the nature of a particular killer, and then studied how the Bible corrects the hazardous tendencies. During that time, it caused great self-evaluation for myself and created some beneficial dialogue as a team.

Each of these worship team killers has an answer. For every problem, there is solution.

1. The solution to pride is **humility**.
2. The solution to inconsistency is **integrity**.
3. The solution to incapability is **excellence**.
4. The solution to detachment is **availability**.
5. The solution to division is **unity**.

Throughout the time of our development, I often shared some of the things I was teaching through weekly blog posts. The main reason I blogged on these topics was for the benefit of those who weren't present at rehearsal on that specific weekly rotation. As we talked through a big issue, I wanted to make sure every single team member had the opportunity to engage with the biblical truth we had wrestled together at the beginning of practice.

Those posts led other pastors to call me. While I have never been an expert on the subject, I think the similar dilemma struck a chord with other leaders. I spent many hours on the phone or over a meal discussing how to develop and disciple worship teams. I was honored to have opportunities to speak at some worship conferences and consult with different churches. At many of those gatherings, I simply walked through the five worship team killers, and after every event, someone would comment, "This material is exactly what our team needed to hear! Have you ever thought about making this a book that a team could go through together?"

I hadn't, but after enough repeated requests, I decided to reconsider. Plenty of great worship resources exist. This volume will not replace any of them. The majority of those volumes are directed towards worship pastors which makes logical sense, but oftentimes, the content is geared towards leading services instead of leading servants. I looked for a resource that could help equip a worship team and not just resource a worship pastor. Since I couldn't find one exactly like the one for which I was looking, I revised my original thinking and wrote these concepts down for others to work through together.

My prayer is that this volume will serve you and your team well. Maybe you read this on your own and it convicts your soul in a specific area. Possibly your choir, band, or tech team reads a chapter a week and discusses the content when you gather together. Perhaps you read it and realize your team is already there and you celebrate how far you have come. In any possible way that this book can make your team make much of Jesus, I will be thrilled!

During the initial time when our team and other ministries went through this material, one question nagged me incessantly:

If others follow my lead, where will they end up?

If you are a worship pastor or part of the worship team at your church, pray about how you and your team can grow in the coming days. Where are the areas of opportunity? What deserves to be challenged? If your team and their offerings are perfect, then don't change a thing. But if there is room to develop, which direction are you heading?

Most importantly, are you really cognizant of what is at stake here?

The Target on Your Back

Your worship team is under spiritual attack. If your team doesn't seem to be besieged, it may be because the battle is already over. You've lost. As believers, you must understand that you are at war. You aren't wrestling against flesh and blood but against spiritual powers (Eph 6:12). Strongholds are being setup inside you and all around you, and if you want your worship ministry to survive, you must take up arms and fight (2 Cor 10:3-4).

If you want to resist the devil and watch him flee from the work of your church, you first must submit to God (James 4:7). In case you feel unsure if he is at work in your context, it is because he is really good at what he does. Prowling around like a roaring lion, the devil seeks to gobble up your entire team one by one (1 Pet 5:8).

In a corporate gathering of worshipers, the people are supposed to respond to revelation. The people receive the revelation of God through the Word and respond to God through worship. All hell trembles when the people of God make much of God. If Satan can water that time down and attack those leaders, there is little work left to do within that congregation.

If you were the enemy of God, where else would you focus your schemes than on those who are supposed to point people to Jesus? If you could get the worship leaders, including the preacher (who is a worship leader), to shine a light on themselves instead of Jesus, you would wreak unimaginable havoc on what could happen in the life of that particular congregation. As a member of the worship team, you are a target.

Since you are a target, would you take some time to research the enemy's strategy? Study through the common assaults and observe the wreckage on the roadside. And then allow the Word and the Spirit to work in your life to ensure you won't be another casualty.

1. PRIDE

Pride goes before destruction, and a haughty spirit before a fall (Prov 16:18).

The first worship team killer is pride. More worship leaders and worship teams have fallen to pride than to any of the other killers. What is unique about pride is that it is a silent killer. Pride uses guerrilla tactics and fights from within the camp. While external catalysts may increase pride, they cannot create it. Pride grows within the heart of the worship leader and sabotages the whole offering. With pride, I actually become the enemy.

A prideful heart is an abomination to the LORD (Prov 16:5) and can bring disgrace (Prov 11:2). While pride attempts to position you high, it actually brings you low (Prov 29:23). Pride encourages us to deceive ourselves by thinking we are something when actually we amount to nothing (Gal

6:3). The irony of pride is that it causes us to esteem ourselves in our own eyes which is a hopeless pursuit (Prov 26:12).

Worship leading is a dangerous task. Concerning the musical side of worship gatherings, churches and ministries assemble teams with a unique charge. Worship teams are the only type of musical producers in the world who are expected to give a quality offering without desiring a commending response.

In every other setting in life, musical presentations are often meant for the applause of those listening. Whether it is your child's piano recital, the community chorale, the symphonic orchestra, or the latest popular band, all of these musical offerings are meant to gather fans, support, and ovation.

In worship, we commission a team of quality musicians to stand upon a physical platform and yet expect them not to slide onto a mental platform.

The challenge is great, the setting is unique, but the warning is urgent. Pride will kill your worship team. In fact, pride is the guaranteed factor that will precipitate your worship ministry's destruction (Prov 16:18) and bring dishonor to the ministry you lead (Prov 11:2).

What's even worse than that tragic reality is that pride on a worship team can actually hinder the worship of an entire congregation. If done poorly, a worship team can use all of their energies for shining a spotlight on themselves rather than God. If I shine the spotlight on myself in worship, I am attempting to rob God of the glory deserving him (Isa 42:8), providing an unworthy object on which others can focus (Gal 6:3), and doing a disservice to those I am leading (Phil 3:17). On the other side, if our efforts are done well, people will notice in such a way not to praise us but to praise God (Matt 5:16).

Unfortunately, our hearts are desperately wicked (Jer 17:9). We struggle not because there are evil desires on the outside of us but on the inside of us (James 4:1). If I fail to acknowledge that I am the problem, there is no solution.

The Manifestation of Pride

While there are many evidences of pride in a worship team, certain cases of it are more regular. How does pride manifest itself in most worship teams?

1. **Desire for Approval** - Every single person is consumed with the longing for approval. In worship leading, we know that we are supposed to fight against that tendency, but it is a difficult position to achieve. You may seem like you are working for the approval of God but are actually seeking the approval of man (1 Cor 4:3). When complimented, you may point your finger towards the heavens and say, "it's God," but if those mannerisms are not reflective in your heart, people may think that you are humble, but God thinks that you are a liar (Prov 12:22; 19:9) and doesn't want you in his house anymore (Ps 101:7). Seek the approval of God rather than man (Gal

1:10). Musical excellence impresses man; personal integrity impresses God.

2. **Craving for Prominence** - The yearning for the solo, the hankering for the first chair, or the appetite for the front row are danger signs. Your gifts do need to be utilized for the building up of the Body of Christ (Eph 4:16), but your gifts don't have to be on display for all the people in order for them to minister to some of the people. If you are craving for prominence, your heart reveals it by a growing desire to be first, noticed, and praised. In the kingdom, the first will be last (Matt 10:16). If all you are seeking is the praise of men, don't expect to receive the praise of God (Matt 6:1). Too often we love the glory from man more than the glory that can only come from God (John 12:43).

3. **Planning for Recognition** - How you select songs and keys for worship say something about your intention. Most recorded worship music is arranged around a vocal soloist and so the song's tonal key highlights that particular individual's awe-inspiring range. The majority of popular worship music is sung in a higher register than the average listener can sing. When a tenor worship leader leads a song in the original key, most of the men in the congregation can't reach the higher notes, and most of the women have to sing those notes in the lower "gutter" part of their range. If you lower the key from the original, your singers won't sound as jaw-dropping as the recording, but

the congregation just might! The goal is to get the congregation to sing to the LORD (Ps 48:1) and to one another (Col 3:16) – not just to hear you sing. Prideful musical selections can actually rob the congregation of their ability to join in with the worship.

4. **Competition with Others** - The craving for prominence naturally leads to competition with others on the team and creates disorder (James 3:16). Arrogance always leads to strife (Prov 13:10). You must learn how to put the desires of others before your own (Phil 2:3-4). Begrudgingly offering opportunities to others may appear as a humble sacrifice, but if it is done without love, it is considered worthless (1 Cor 13:3). If you can't celebrate the contributions of others on the team because of your own jealousy (1 Cor 3:3), pride is taking over your soul. Do you honestly celebrate the contributions of your team members or are you constantly thinking of how you could have done it better?

There are many other manifestations of pride on a worship team, and they can be ever so subtle and yet so dangerous. In some ways, pride is the greatest secret danger on a worship team because we can hide it so well. Since it is so subtle, is there anything we can do about it? Should we even try to address it or is it just an expected part of the environment?

You must realize this: God is not mocked. Whatever a man sows, this he will reap (Gal 6:7). God will not allow pride to continue to go unchecked. Pride on your worship team will be addressed one way or the other.

If you don't humble yourself, God will.

Worship Team Opposition

Since worship music is a lightning rod for controversy in local churches, worship teams are very familiar with hostile opposition. From the lady with her arms crossed during a particular type of worship song, to the man with his hands over his ears when those devilish drums start, to the staunch purist who scoffs at anything sung that is not in his preferential lyrical realm, to the anonymous pen pal that threatens the leader concerning all things done poorly, worship teams are no stranger to antagonism. You think you know opposition, but even the best of those aforementioned opponents are nothing to be concerned about. There is a greater nemesis at hand.

You don't know what opposition is until you have experienced the hand of God against you.

And guess what? If pride remains ungoverned, the least of your concerns is the critics in your church. The Almighty God is against you. Prepare for that bout. He opposes the proud (James 4:6; 1 Pet 5:5). He tears down the homes of the prideful (Prov 15:25). He keeps the lofty at a distance (Ps 138:6). An arrogant heart is an abomination to the LORD and he has promised to punish such treason (Prov 16:5).

God will not share his glory with another, and if you are trying to take it from him, mark my words – you will lose this fight.

Learn what it means to humble yourselves and do it quickly (1 Pet 5:6; James 4:10; Mic 6:8; Matt 23:12). Worship teams, humble yourselves before God does it for you.

The story in 2 Chronicles 26 is chilling. Uzziah is King in Judah who originally "set himself to seek God" (2 Chron 26:5). It says that "God helped him" (2 Chron 26:7) in many amazing tasks as king. And as "long as he sought the LORD, God made him prosper" (2 Chron 26:5).

But there arose a problem. This next line is one of the most intense phrases in the Bible because it reveals so much concerning our oblivious nature to the actual conditions of our hearts. It says that "he was marvelously helped until he was strong. But when he was strong, he grew proud, to his destruction" (2 Chron 26:15-16).

That's the problem with many worship leaders and Christians in general. We have been marvelously helped, and we continue to be marvelously helped until we become strong in our own eyes and think we are somebody. We think we deserve something. We think we are truly significant. We begin to think that we can't be replaced. Pride blinds us to many essential truths.

- Never forget that all the good we have has been received (1 Cor 4:7).
- We are mere jars of clay molded together in order to possess God's power (2 Cor 4:7).

- Even if we did everything commanded of us we are still only able to be called "worthless slaves" (Luke 17:10).
- We don't possess anything that we didn't receive from heaven (John 3:27).
- All things come from God (1 Chron 29:14).
- Anything good in us or around us comes from God (James 1:17).

God marvelously helps us, and at some point, we forget that truth.

With success comes baggage. We begin to think we have arrived. We honestly believe that we deserve what we have, and we neglect to thank God. In those times, it is not beyond God to say, "So you think that you don't need me and you can do it all on your own? Let's see how you do if I remove my hand of blessing from your ministry. I won't marvelously help you anymore."

The tragedy is that most of us never see it coming. We have hit a certain stride and believe that God is blessing our incredibly remarkable efforts. The danger is that so many of us are experiencing natural success and thinking it is being guided by a supernatural blessing. We never realize that God is the only good we have (Ps 16:2). In our ignorance, we continue our pathetic efforts to do something of significance only later to find out that the only times when our works ever amounted to anything is when we were marvelously helped. Pride goes before destruction, and a haughty spirit before a fall (Prov 16:18). We must walk so carefully.

Humility – Lead With Perspective

If pride is the number one worship team killer, then what is the answer? The solution is humility. Humble worship leaders are servants who are able to lead with perspective. Once you alter your perception and understand that you are nothing and God is everything, worship leading becomes simple. Honestly, all of life becomes simple when you humble yourself. He becomes great, you become less. He must increase, you must decrease (John 3:30).

Humility is a tricky value to possess. Once you think you have acquired it, you have already lost it. We are to aspire to humility but never act as if we have acquired it.

The complexity of humility is seen well in the life of Moses. Moses escaped an ethnic cleansing (Ex 2:3), trained in Pharaoh's family (Ex 2:10), brandished his personal strength in order to redeem his kinsmen (Ex 2:12), confronted Pharaoh through miraculous signs (Ex 4:21), directed the people through the parted Red Sea (Ex 14:29), received the Ten Commandments from the hands of God (Ex 31:18), and led the stubborn Israelites up to the cusp of the Promised Land (Deut 34:3). Few ministry résumés exist with more clout than the list of accomplishments mentioned in Moses' history. Given this type of experience, Moses could have easily struggled with pride.

Contrastingly, Moses' life was marked more with humility than pride. It is written that "the man Moses was very humble, more than any man who was on the face of the earth" (Num 12:3). The hilarity of that verse is that many translations have the entire verse contained within parentheses because most scholars believe that Moses wrote the Book of Numbers! Certain commentators believe that the verse must be an editorial comment because as soon as you write that you are the most humble person in the whole world you just became the most prideful person in the whole world.

At another time, you can wrestle with the philosophical discussion concerning whether or not the most humble person could accurately write such a statement without disqualifying themselves, but the main takeaway is this: the closer you encounter God, the more humble you become. If Moses had been a part of so many incredible moments, how could he remain so humble? Simple. He knew the LORD face to face (Deut 34:10).

His proximity to the LORD kept his position in perspective.

Moses wasn't the only one like this however. Righteous Job covered his mouth speechless when he finally encountered God whom he so eagerly desired to question (Job 40:4). The presence of God made Joshua the commander on the eve of battle fall on his face and worship (Josh 5:14). King David marveled that God would even think about creatures as small as himself (Ps 8:3-4). King Solomon, the richest and most successful leader in Israel, saw himself in the presence of God as a little child unable to discern the simplest of tasks (1 Kings 3:7). After experiencing the LORD high and lifted up (Isa 6:1), Isaiah didn't feel better about himself but feared for his safety due to his sinful condition (Isa 6:5).

These examples from the great cloud of witnesses (Heb 12:1) are just a sampling. When people encountered God in the Old Testament and the New Testament, they rarely walked away thinking highly of themselves. In fact, they rarely thought of themselves at all.

Their gaze had been set on another much more magnificent and had displaced the need to focus upon themselves any longer.

Most people attempt to exalt themselves in one way or another. Jesus once again breaks the paradigm by teaching that servant leaders don't position themselves for exaltation. They do their job and allow God to do the positioning. Jesus taught that someone should not even desire to sit at the head table but instead seek out the lowliest place possible (Luke 14:8).

Nearing his death, Jesus even taught his disciples that no one should even aspire to an office of leadership (Matt 23:10). He taught the need to be faithful in the small things and to be trusting in the big things. Combatting the Pharisees who thought that their efforts earned them special places of leadership in God's eyes, Jesus actually opposed the very desire to be a leader based on one's perceived qualifications. Jesus stated, "Whoever exalts himself shall be humbled; and whoever humbles himself shall be exalted" (Matt 23:12). The totality of Scripture affirms Jesus' statement.

God can and will dramatically humble those who try to promote themselves.

As Jesus humbly washed his disciples' feet during the Last Supper (John 13:5-20), he exemplified true humility. Not only was it an unthinkable, lowly task, omniscient Jesus willfully washed the feet of Judas who would soon betray him (John 18:1-9), Peter who would deny him (John 18:25-27), and the remaining ten disciples who would abandon him in the crucial coming hours (Matt 26:56).

If Jesus, who did not regard equality with God as something to be grasped (Phil 2:6), could humble himself, should it really be that difficult for someone like me to humble myself? Humility should be the natural response to encountering Christ. If I truly encounter Jesus, how can I not be humble?

Humbly on Display

Humility is not something you attempt to display but you do strive to portray. The humble leader will not feel the need to be noticed, but humility will inevitably be noticed because it is such a rarity in our world. Other humble people can recognize humility and rejoice (Ps 34:2). The humble don't need to seek praise because God sends others to esteem them (Prov 27:2), and God himself exalts the humble (Matt 23:12; Job 22:29; Prov 29:23; Luke 14:11; 18:14; James 4:6; 1 Pet 5:6).

Whenever we serve in a manner to get attention for ourselves, we are attempting to rob God of his glory.

People who are called to lead others in worship must be fervently attempting to lead humbly before God and his people. In the humility department of leading worship, four things are absolutely essential:

1. **Genuine Faith** - To lead in worship, one must be confident of one's own salvation in Jesus Christ. If you are truly aware of what your salvation cost, you should never feel as if you deserve any recognition for anything you do. The gospel reminds us that no good works were necessary or even present in our lives in order for us to earn anything (Rom 5:6-8; Gal 2:21; Eph 2:8-9; 1 Tim 1:15; Titus 3:5). Possessing genuine faith helps you remain in awe that Jesus would love someone as helpless as you.

2. **Correct Doctrine** - In order to lead biblical worship, one must possess correct biblical doctrine concerning essential truths (the Bible, God, Mankind, Jesus, the Holy Spirit, Salvation, the Church, and Eternity). If your team is going to lead songs that are supposed to teach truth (Col 3:16), you need to make sure your team is devoted to God's Word (Josh 1:8; Ps 119:131) and understands good theology (1 Tim 4:6; 2 Tim 1:13; 4:3; Titus 1:9; 2:1, 10; 2 John 1:9)! A correct understanding of God leads to deeper worship. As a worship leader, you should pray that you would continually be sanctified in the truth of God's Word (John 17:17).

3. **Proper Intentions** - While pride will be a struggle for every believer, each member of this team must have proper intentions of leading boldly on stage and off

stage for the purpose of pointing people to Jesus. We must make war with our pride and test our own actions (1 Cor 4:6). If you seek an audience of anyone other than Jesus, worship ministry is not for you. You are not supposed to lead in a way that seeks a spotlight on you. Your leading should direct the spotlight towards Jesus. If you don't humble yourself, rest assured that God will do it for you (Lev 26:19; Obad 1:3-4; 2 Chron 26:16; Job 40:11; Prov 16:5; Isa 2:11-12; 13:11; 23:9).

4. **Humble Disposition** - My prideful heart tries to convince my mind that I am the best person on the team. Even if the improbable chance of my ideas always being the best were true (which they are not), my attitude needs to be one of service and selflessness (Matt 20:26; Rom 12:10; Phil 2:3-5). My perspective must shift. Not only do I need to realize this truth, but others need to believe that about me. It's important what I say and how I say it. I must acknowledge and even portray that:

- I am not the most *brilliant* person on the team.
- I am not the most *creative* person on the team.
- I am not the most *talented* person on the team.

Your ministry would go further faster if you would realize that you are not the center of the universe. If you keep God in his proper central place, everything else orbits much better.

Facedown

Humility should be a prerequisite of authentic worship. True worship isn't supposed to lift us up; it is supposed to bring us facedown. In Revelation 4, the Apostle John saw a vision of heaven in which the twenty-four elders were seated on their own personal thrones arrayed in heavenly attire. "Around the throne were twenty-four thrones, and seated on the thrones were twenty-four elders, clothed in white garments, with golden crowns on their heads" (Rev. 4:4). Who are these 24 elders? While there are plenty of theories concerning their identity, I believe they are meant to show the unity between Old Testament and New Testament believers. Quite possibly, these thrones are reserved for representing the twelve sons of Israel (Rev 21:12) and the twelve apostles of the Lamb (Rev 21:14).

Whoever these people are, they possess an unthinkable privilege of having a significant throne and a shiny crown in none other than the heavenlies (Rev 4:4). If you have the opportunity to sit upon a throne in heaven of all places, it's fair to say that someone has esteemed you rather highly. It would also be difficult for me to imagine that you could have that status and not be tempted to wrestle with pride. Out of all the nations and throughout all of history, these twenty-four elders are favored enough to sit on a throne in the middle of the heavenly congregation. When you get your own throne in the grand throne room of heaven, you have officially arrived.

In fact, it does appear that these people are of great significance until someone of greater significance arrives.

These elders of high position lose their esteemed status in the presence of God.

"And whenever the living creatures give glory and honor and thanks to him who is seated on the throne, who lives forever and ever, the twenty-four elders fall down before him who is seated on the throne and worship him who lives forever and ever. They cast their crowns before the throne, saying, 'Worthy are you, our Lord and God, to receive glory and honor and power, for you created all things, and by your will they existed and were created'" (Rev 4:9-11).

Only One Worthy

In worship leadership, there is a sense of dignity associated with the role. Right or wrong, people can put those on an elevated stage upon imaginary thrones. They expect more out of the worship leaders, but if we are not careful, we will let our God-given mantle of leadership turn us into prideful people.

We may feel like we are somebody, but that premonition should flee the moment when Jesus walks into the room. In that moment, we shouldn't feel compelled for anything other than falling facedown. In those moments, let us remember that the only one worthy is Jesus!

Even though we have the privilege to lead others in worship, we bear it with responsibility and therefore lead with perspective. We lead with humility. We are in the presence of the King of all kings (Rev 1:5; 17:14; 19:16). We shouldn't envision that he is honored we came into his presence. We should be honored that we could even be allowed into his presence.

True worship should humble you rather than esteem you.

It is an easy trap for gifted people to turn into entitled people. Looking upon our status in the worship gathering, we can begin to believe that we deserve our seats and our crowns. If not careful, we can believe the lie that we made our gifts rather than received our gifts (1 Cor 4:7). The assassin of pride is so dangerous because God proactively opposes prideful worship teams (James 4:6). If we honestly grasp our condition in light of the holiness of God, pride should be found killed than it be found killing us.

Do you tremble in the presence of God anymore? Are you amazed that he even allows you to worship? The greatest way to combat your pride is to draw near to the Lord.

As we've discussed the dangers of pride and the glories of humility, your mind has probably drifted towards someone on your team that you hope has read this chapter by now. You might even be praying that it knocks some sense into their prideful, stubborn hearts.

If you are hoping that somebody else got the gist of this chapter, you have already missed the entire point.

In fact, you might be in danger of the worst kind of pride – the version of it that goes unnoticed. Be careful. Pride brings down the mighty (Prov 16:18). Let anyone who thinks that he stands take heed lest he fall (1 Cor 10:12).

2. INCONSISTENCY

Whoever walks in integrity walks securely, but he who makes his ways crooked will be found out (Prov 10:9).

The second worship team killer is inconsistency. Leading with a lack of integrity attempts to portray a false sense of holiness. We are in serious danger when our external expressions are far more dedicated than our internal devotion. Trying to create a fidelity facade attempts to deceive others (2 Tim 3:13) but actually deceives oneself (Rom 7:11; James 1:16, 22, 26). There is only one who is not deceived concerning personal inconsistency – God. While we may strive to create a pious persona in front of others, God sees straight through it to who we truly are (Prov 15:11; Jer 20:12; John 2:25; Acts 15:8).

Our stage portrayal should not be a soul betrayal.

As worship leaders, we must fight against inconsistency. How our congregation sees us on stage should not fluctuate from who we truly are off the stage. Those who dwell with the Lord must possess a sense of integrity (Ps 15:1-2). The LORD despises worship from a talented mouth that cannot be backed with a sincere heart (Isa 29:13). While we are called to lead others, our public worship should never exceed our private devotion. Worship should be an overflow from our hearts (Matt 12:34), and we must never desire our holiness to be noticed by others which provides a lesser reward (Matt 6:5-6) and devalues why we strive for integrity.

Where Integrity Lacks

Over the years, I've been able to lead some incredible worship gatherings. Whether I was singing, preaching, or organizing the services, I have valued putting a great deal of intentionality into every offering. As a result, I think a lot about the prospect of a person only coming to one worship service and never to return again. What would we portray to that individual during that one service?

This kind of thought process causes me to strive for a level of intentional excellence in the way we lead worship gatherings at every opportunity. One day, I was forced to think of another important scenario with far deeper implications. Instead of concerning myself with an excellence in the way we led, I was forced to think about an excellence in the way we lived.

In one ministry season, I bumped into a casual acquaintance and realized that she had been absent from our worship gatherings as of late. I knew she loved Jesus and was very ministry minded, so I honestly became immediately concerned that I had not seen her in a while. Was our band getting stale? Was the production lackluster? Was there a better option in town? Was the preaching off? While I try not to think that technical, I understand people, and so my mind wandered all over the place.

"Hey, I don't want this question to be awkward, but I have to ask you something. I haven't seen you in a while at our worship gathering. Is everything OK?"

"Yeah, I'm doing great, but I will never come back there again."

"OK. Can I ask you why?"

"Sure. I can't come and worship with a group of people who allow one of the worship leaders to continue in an adulterous relationship."

I was shocked. I was confused. I was defensive. Whoever she was talking about, I knew her information had to be wrong. There is no way something like this could be happening in a ministry I was watching over. I tried to assure her concerning the unreliability of rumors but promised that I would check into it myself.

While it was necessary that I investigated the situation, I was regrettably wrong about my assumptions. The confrontation was a painful process, because I found out that this person (and probably many more like this person) had a legitimate reason to avoid our worship services – we weren't taking leadership integrity seriously. When I confronted the team member, the allegation was denied but the defendant seemed very uneasy when I started probing.

I couldn't let it go. Eventually, I got to the truth, and the truth wasn't pretty. In fact, this event and others in the surrounding months caused me to believe vehemently in the phrase, "where there's smoke, there's fire." When I looked back over the recent months, clues were all around. My intuition told me something was off, but I remained naïve that someone like this could do something like that. In reality, this team member was transgressing in more than just the original claim.

I realized that if there is smoke in ministry, there is most likely a fire blazing nearby.

For a few weeks, we led worship with an incomplete band. Some of the congregation probably knew that I had to confront one of the band members, but many others never gave the changeup a second thought. During that time, our musical quality wasn't as sharp as it had been but our honorable quality was never more on point. If I'm honest, while the technicalities seemed more labored, the spirituality felt more natural. Why was that? I think God takes the character of worship leaders more important that we can imagine.

Hypocritical Worship Leaders

Those who lead in worship are responsible for holding themselves to a high standard. We stand before congregations representing the holiness of Jesus and the reputation of the church. What people see in worship leaders, they tend to generalize about that particular fellowship of believers.

What people see on Sunday mornings should be what they would discover in us on Monday through Saturday as well.

Our entire lives must be committed to God – not just a few hours a week. While none of us can live perfectly yet (Matt 5:48; 2 Cor 3:18; Rev 21:27), we must strive towards personal holiness (Matt 5:8; Rom 6:22; Heb 12:14). As those who are called to leading others to a greater degree of personal holiness, we must labor relentlessly with the power that God provides (Rom 12:3; 1 Cor 15:10; 2 Cor 13:4; Phil 2:12-13; Heb 13:21) to align our reputation with our character.

If your reputation and character don't match up, you are a hypocrite.

I can remember exactly where I was when I heard that line. Francis Chan was teaching a group of adult leaders at a Passion Conference. When you attend a conference like Passion, you feel like you are attempting to take a sip of water from a fire hydrant. It is an enormous amount of solid content coming your direction all day and night. Out of all the teaching that I heard that week, the following exercise lingered in my mind years after the event.

Chan had all the leaders present make two columns on a piece of paper. On the left side, he asked us to make a list of adjectives that people in our churches or ministries would use to describe us. In the right column, he told us to make a list of adjectives that God would use to describe us.

1. What *people* say about me is my **reputation**.
2. What *God* says about me is my **character**.

After compiling both lists, he asked us to examine and compare both columns. If the two lists didn't match up, we were in a problematic position. For if people say one thing about you and God would say another, that means the people in your life don't really know you. They know a make-believe version of you but they don't know the real you. People who are more concerned with reputation than character are those who are on their best behavior when others are around.

If your reputation and character don't match up, you are a hypocrite. When I heard those words, I was crushed. I reasoned that my reputation was pretty solid in people's eyes, but God, who knows every single action, word, and thought, could portray a completely different person.

Unfortunately, all of us live two lives to some extent. I have the life that God sees, and I have the life that everyone else sees. As leaders in a worship ministry, we must strive to have our reputation and character match.

The people we are leading need to have leaders who exemplify integrity.

When we lead in worship and declare God is holy, do we take our own holiness seriously? If we sing that we will follow wherever God leads us, do our footprints testify to that promise? Do we act a certain way in front of the church and act a different in front of our family?

If I'm honest, I'm marred with inconsistency. I care more for my reputation than my character. I can't stand to think you may look down on me but forget about the one who actually is looking down on me. Regardless of how polished I am at my worship leading craft, if my life is a far cry from the holiness I claim to possess, I am a fake.

Credibility - Leading with Integrity

If inconsistency is the problem, what is the solution? It's credibility. The worship leader who works for credibility is able to lead the congregation with integrity.

As people of the LORD, our integrity is supposed to be a notable characteristic of our lives (Prov 11:3; 12:22; 20:7). As worship leaders, we will be slandered, but our good behavior should put our slanderers to shame (1 Pet 3:16) as we portray God's kindness and patience with those adversaries in our lives (2 Tim 2:23-26). More than any sacrificial commitment to excellence or offering, the LORD is pleased far more with righteousness and justice (Prov 21:3). God takes integrity seriously.

Before going further, I want to address a pushback that might be entering your mind. I want to warn you about falling into one of two ditches on either side of the narrow road of biblical Christianity (Matt 7:14). You might be thinking that no one is perfect besides Jesus and you would be right, but Jesus' perfection is not a free pass for you to rebel against everything he stands for.

Here's the danger. Many people have fallen into a ditch on one side called legalism. It's a trap to make someone do good works in order to earn God's approval. That's not the gospel.

I think because so many people and churches hated the legalism ditch so much, they overcompensated and swerved to the opposite side of the road into another ditch called easy-believism. This cheap grace is a trap that makes people believe that Jesus loves them so much that they never have to change.

Biblical Christianity is different. Jesus taught about the narrow road of biblical salvation. It teaches that we are saved by grace (Eph 2:8-9), but that grace changes us in order to do good works (Eph 2:10).

We are not saved by good works – we are saved for good works.

To help you understand, let me remind you of three important theological terms:

1. **Justification** - the declaration of holiness
2. **Sanctification** - the process of holiness
3. **Glorification** - the completion of holiness

Justification is celebrated the day you receive the gospel and God declares you not-guilty. Glorification is commemorated the day when you finally meet Jesus face to face and don't have to worry about sin anymore. We remember justification, we anticipate glorification, but we are neglecting sanctification.

Sanctification is the process of holiness that is worked on from the day you receive the gospel until the day you see the author of the gospel. This process is the heart of discipleship. While justification and sanctification are completely the work of the Lord, sanctification is the work of the Lord and us. Sanctification is hard work and will not be complete until we die.

The proof that we are neglecting sanctification is the lack of holiness present in many Christians. Simply put: there is little change in our lives. If you did a review over the last few years, you might not notice any progress.

If there is a true profession of faith, there should be a true progression of faith.

Jesus didn't die for you to continue in sin. He doesn't expect you to maintain a passive aggressive rebellion. He expects you to move past the lame excuse that you can't help your sinful condition because you are simply "a sinner saved by grace." When I defend myself by saying "that's just the way I am," I am faulting God for my mistake. Within our natural tendencies, we must not neglect the power of God to change us. He is not through with us yet (Phil 1:6).

Instead of defending your words or actions by saying," that's just the way I am," maybe you should start progressing in your walk and proclaiming, "that's just the way I was!" Your past does not define you. Your sinful personality does not define you. God defines you, and he is not done with you yet.

Higher Standard

The reason this concept is so important to understand as a worship leader is that while salvation is given, integrity is not. Credibility takes time and effort. Christians are expected to live by a higher standard (Rom 12:1; Eph 2:10; 4:1; Phil 1:27; Col 1:10; 1 Thess 2:12; 4:1), and Christian leaders such as elders (1 Tim 3:2; Titus 1:6), deacons (1 Tim 3:10), and teachers (James 3:1) are expected to live by even a higher standard than the previously mentioned high standard.

We don't strive for integrity in order to earn God's love but because we already have it.

Those who lead in worship are responsible for holding themselves to a high standard. We stand before congregations representing the church and teach others by the manner in which we lead (Col 3:16). As people who visibly represent the church in front of the congregation, we must realize that people will hold us to a higher standard. What people see in us, they tend to generalize about our fellowship of believers. People deserve to see the same worshiper on Monday through Saturday that they see on Sunday. Leading with integrity is so important because people don't need any more reasons to believe Christians are hypocrites.

Our entire lives must be committed to God and not just a few hours a week. While none of us can live in that manner perfectly, we must aim towards perfection (Matt 5:48) of holiness because our Father is holy (1 Pet 1:16). God desires your obedience more than your sacrifice (1 Sam 15:22).

As a worship leader, you must work on more than what others see of you when you are on a stage. If you desire tangible results, work solely on physical matters. If you desire eternal results, then you must also work on spiritual matters.

If you desire to take your worship leadership to another level of effectiveness, evaluate how you are doing in the following four essential areas for establishing worship leading credibility:

1. **Personal Life** - Is there anything in your life that would keep someone from following your lead in worship? Could someone walk in the front door, see you leading in worship, and question the credibility of the entire congregation? There isn't much that is personal when you are in the public eye. Your life is your life – all of it. Distinctions fade away when you decide to lead. There isn't the personal side, the work side, the religious side, etc. It's all about God or it's not. What we may think is hidden can easily be discovered. We must strive to live a genuine life committed to Christ in every area. Love God. Love others. Be intentional with your life and be Kingdom-focused in your pursuits. We are the

ambassadors for Christ in this world – live like it (2 Co. 5:20).

2. **Private Worship** - Our public worship should never exceed our private devotion. If worship does not come from the overflow of our hearts (Matt. 12:34), then we are in danger of trying to put on a show. If I am more expressive in public, my intentions might be for the public's approval. If worship is an offering to the LORD, then why would my gift look any different when others are around? Do you sing worship more on stage or off stage? Are you in God's Word more in a service or outside a service? Is the only time you pray when you are gathered with other believers? Our public worship should serve as a "public display of affection" but never replace our personal intimacy with Jesus. I value offering outward expressions during corporate worship, but I also believe there is something special about when we do something that only God sees. In those offerings, it is hard to doubt authenticity.

3. **Particular Relationships** - While your conduct should be outstanding among all people (1 Pet. 2:12; Matt. 5:16) and especially to those of the household of faith (Gal. 6:10), there are particular relationships that are of utmost importance. The people who see you close will know you best. How is the spiritual health of your family? If I cannot lead my own family in worship, what business do I have with leading another family in worship? Our families know us best, and they deserve our best. If familial relationships are in

danger, you are responsible to put all of your efforts there instead of investing on a ministry team. Just as the biblical qualifications for elders require a man to be devoted to his wife (1 Tim 3:2; Titus 1:6) and have disciplined children (1 Tim 3:4-5; Titus 1:6), we must also provide such an example for those in our church fellowship. The Christian life cannot be compartmentalized.

4. **Physical Appearance** - We live in a culture that provides enough variety in clothing to show your style without having to show anything else. You have freedom to be trendy as long as it isn't tempting. People can actually be stylish and appropriate at the same time. By dressing modestly, we acknowledge that our bodies are a temple of the Holy Spirit (1 Cor 6:19-20) and attempt to remove stumbling blocks (Rom.14:13; 1 Cor 8:9; 1 John 2:10) from the path of your brothers and sisters in Christ. While your clothing shouldn't have a different standard if you are on or off the stage, realize that being on a platform causes all eyes to look at you. Don't give them a reason to show you attention other than the fact that you are pointing them to behold the LORD. Is your clothing neat (this has more to do with sloppiness than style), non-distractive (why would clothing beg for attention when we desire them to focus on Jesus), and modest (nothing too revealing or too tight). It is an awkward conversation to have when you have to send someone home to change wardrobes, but the important task of leading worship makes the discomfort worth it.

While there are plenty of components for worship leaders, these four essentials are often overlooked because they are not easily witnessed. Even if others can't see your heart in these four areas, God does. Seek to please him.

Inconsistency Outruns Ability

No level of skill can compensate for a lack of integrity. I learned this tangibly as we enrolled my sons into flag football when they turned eight years old. My reservations for the league were confirmed when I was given a code of conduct, not for the players, but for the parents! Thankfully, we didn't collect too many bizarre stories that first year. While their record was not stellar that season, I loved watching my sons be in a losing situation and still having the time of their lives.

In a close game, one of my sons caught a pass and took off for the end zone. As he turned on the jets, he left everyone in his dust. The crowd was cheering and a touchdown seemed imminent, until I see his flag fly up in the air near the end zone. As I attempted to determine from my vantage point who was even close enough to extend to such a length to catch him on the one-yard line, another parent informed me that no one was close enough to get his flag. He accidentally knocked it out himself. He was running so hard that the only person who could stop him was himself.

I have seen this scenario play out too often in ministry contexts. People traveling at such a great speed with so much success, and the only person close enough to slow them down is themselves. It happens time and time again. Too many people take themselves out of the game because they pull their own flags.

1. If you think you are standing strong, be careful that you aren't blind to a possible fall (1 Cor 10:12).

2. People who walk in crooked ways will always be found out (Prov 10:9).

3. Corrupt ways are normally what destroys a person (Prov 11:3).

4. We are supposed to live honorably in front of people but in such a way that our reputation matches our character (1 Pet 2:12; 2 Cor 8:21; 1 Pet 3:16).

5. Those who dwell with God are those who live with integrity (Ps 15:1-2).

6. If we lack obedience to our convictions, we aren't deceiving others – we deceive ourselves (James 1:22-25).

7. Your war is often not with external forces but with internal forces (James 4:1).

You probably are very talented. Your giftedness has probably opened up many doors for you. Realize though that you might be at a place where your greatest enemy is yourself.

Your talent can take you to a place where your character can't keep you.

You may be beyond the reach of everyone else grabbing your flag that the only person who can remove you from the game is yourself. And that is the worst tragedy of them all.

3. INABILITY

Sing to him a new song; play skillfully on the strings, with loud shouts (Ps 33:3).

The third worship team killer is inability. While pride and inconsistency are character-based inward killers, inability is a skill-related outward killer. Dealing with a lack of quality in worship leading may seem like an awkward and cruel topic to discuss in a church setting, but that is because we have developed an incorrect reasoning for why we attempt to lead with progressive adeptness.

Imagine a scenario that all of us have been a part of at some point in our lives. It is Sunday morning and a vocalist grabs the microphone to share the special music with the congregation. Why is it called "special music?"

The designation is supposed to indicate that this music is different from the rest of the music. In most evangelical settings, it is meant to be a performance by an individual or a group rather than a participation by the congregation. The selection is special indeed, but what makes it special can be for differing reasons.

Sometimes it is *special* because it is *especially* awful to hear. It has nothing to do with whether or not the selection is your style. It is just painful to the auditory sensory faculties. This person has been asked to sing a solo, and you wish he or she was singing so low that you couldn't hear him or her (sorry, I couldn't resist).

Usually when this scenario takes place in a church context, we actually lavish encouraging words on the soloist. Maybe you can classify the lie as an exaggeration, but be forewarned that heaping compliments on the quality of the offering could set your church up for more similar solos in the future. Maybe you reason in your mind that God instructed us to make a joyful noise (Ps 98:4), but you are unsure of how much joy that it is actually producing.

We tend to tolerate mediocre talent in worship because it's "only church."

Since it is an offering to God and church people are supposed to be categorically nice people, we tend to overlook a lack of proficiency. We tend to say that God sees the heart. I could not agree with you more, but we misunderstand what even the word "heart" means. In biblical times, the heart was not the warm and fuzzy organ of the body. The heart was the base of operations for decision-making capabilities within the body. The heart didn't feel what to do; the heart decided what to do. God does see the heart, and if we fail to make up our minds to give our absolute best, he sees that absolutely clearly.

"Sing for joy in the LORD, O you righteous ones; praise is becoming to the upright. Give thanks to the LORD with the lyre; sing praises to him with a harp of ten strings. Sing to him a new song; play skillfully with a shout of joy. For the word of the LORD is upright, and all his work is done in faithfulness" (Ps 33:1-4).

This psalm indicates that righteous people are called to sing praise. Worship leaders must first focus on being righteous before being proficient. Being righteous involves exhibiting both humility and integrity. Additionally, this passage indicates that competence should accompany this type of righteousness.

Musicians are expected to offer their skills to the LORD. In worship environments, it is imperative that singers and musicians lead skillfully at their craft. Why? The psalmist explains that the word of the LORD is upright.

If worship teams are called to declare the truth and goodness of God, they better do it in the best possible manner that they can.

He is deserving of the best we can offer. Unfortunately, the pages of the Bible and the chronicles of our lives tell a completely alternative story. Instead of offering God our best, we often present to him our leftovers. Having already given away everything quantifiably substantive to every other idol in our lives, we simply have nothing left but scraps to offer to the King of kings and the Lord of lords.

The LORD rejected Cain's offering and accepted his brother Abel's offering. It wasn't the type of the offering given but the quality of the offering given in that Abel offered his first – his best to the LORD (Gen 4:3-4; Heb 11:4). Haggai noticed that people had plenty of time and money to spend on their houses but nothing left to spend on God's house (Hag 1:4). The prophet Malachi rebuked the worship leaders of his day for offering their lame and sick animals to the LORD knowing good and well they would never offer such a pitiful gift to any person and yet they offered it none other than God himself (Mal 1:8, 13-14). In fact, God said he would rather have closed the doors to the temple and skipped worship than have them present him their contemptible offerings (Mal 1:10).

After King David had sinned greatly in the pride department (2 Sam 24:10), he wanted to make things right. He was led to assemble an altar at a specific place owned by a man named Araunah (2 Sam 24:18). When Araunah saw King David approaching, he offered his majesty not only the floor to make the sacrifice but also the animals for the sacrifice (2 Sam 24:22). While David could have easily accepted this offer, his response teaches us something significant regarding worship: "No, but I will buy it from you for a price. I will not offer burnt offerings to the LORD my God that cost me nothing" (2 Sam 24:24).

How should worship teams apply this truth? Our worship assemblies are significant gatherings, and we should never just try to "get by" in our offerings. Every musician ought to work at his or her craft. Just because you have natural talent does not mean that you should continue to lead on last year's skills. In offering worship to God and calling people to join in with us, we should never get lazy or stagnate. God gets glory when we work hard with what he has given us (Col 3:23). Our offerings should cost us something!

Work at it, because he is worth it.

Worship leading starts with the heart, but the skills are pivotal as well. Many worship leaders apply little effort to their craft. In fact, if they took the amount of work that they put into their worship leading and applied it to their marriages, schooling, and careers, they would end up divorced, suspended, and fired. Inability is a killer of negligence that reveals to God and your congregation how little you make of worship.

Capability - Leading with Excellence

Worship leaders should desire to lead with excellence. They should strive to maintain and improve their worship leading capabilities. Every musician, vocalist, and technician should desire to lead with continual improvement. We offer our service in this way not to draw people's attention to ourselves, but in order to draw attention to God in an excellent manner.

There is a difference between a gift and a craft. People are born with gifts – they develop crafts.

While your giftedness can take you far, your development of those gifts allows you to maximize your efforts. Worship leading starts with the heart, but the skills are pivotal to the role as well. We are not performing for others, but we are offering our voices and talents to God which means we need to give our best and that our best should always be in the process of getting better.

As you gather a worship team together, depending upon your context, they will have to possess a certain amount of required skills before joining (ability to read music, play with click track, find harmony parts, use Nashville number system, indicate vital signs, etc.). Before they join the team, they might even have a type of audition or screening process.

Once a person is on the team, he or she has not arrived. Each team member should focus on personal development by embracing their gifts and honing their crafts. While there are avenues for seasonal training, each week team members should work diligently in three contexts: 1) individual preparation, 2) group rehearsal, and 3) corporate worship.

Individual Preparation

While most worship teams are composed of volunteers, the weight of this ministry should still hold a high level of accountability concerning preparation. All individual members should be prepared before practice and not use the group time as a cram session.

Corporate cramming sessions serve as an inconsiderate waste of time and an absolute stressful environment for all team members.

Many team members know the disappointing feeling that accompanies a practice with no agenda. When the leader is unprepared, the team is unprepared. As the leader searches for equipment, scrounges for notes, and stretches for explanations, the entire team is tense and each member leaves anxious about the upcoming worship gathering for which they feel no more prepared than they did before the beginning of rehearsal.

Many team leaders know the frustrating feeling that accompanies a practice with no preparatory measures. When obvious transitions are neglected, simple movements are absent, and clear instructions are disregarded, a team leader is ready to quit. While he knows everyone is busy, he really wants each team member to take this calling seriously. It is more than the leader's reputation at stake here – this team is trying to lead others in worship. How can they help prepare others if they are not prepared themselves?

To make sure that practice is efficient and as stress-free as possible, both the leader and the team members need to make commitments to one another. These commitments should be fleshed out in individual preparation time and before group rehearsal.

The worship leader should commit to:

1. **Clear Assignments** - It is rare for a team member to come more prepared than what you have prepared

him or her. While certain personality types will come prepared regardless of the amount of articulated expectations, most members will never surpass what is given. Providing clear assignments for all team members is vital for the team's ability to lead well. In fact, if the leader fails to give clear assignments, oftentimes, the slackers will slack more and the initiative-takers will become frustrated and take the initiative to leave the group. If you are going to lead, then lead with zeal (Rom 12:8). Think through the questions that your team members will have and answer them before they are asked. When you send out requests, send out pertinent details concerning who is leading a part, offering a prayer, or reading a passage. The more precise you are with the group allows the members to receive clear expectations, enjoy smooth practices, and interact with fewer distractions.

2. **Sufficient Leeway** - As the worship leader, you can't enforce that your team will come with a certain level of excellence, but you surely can set them up for a certain level of success. As a pastoral leader, your job is to equip the saints for the work of the ministry (Eph 4:12). In order to do that, you need to give them a sufficient amount of leeway time to prepare. For years, I operated as a last-minute leader because I could pull certain things off on the fly. Once I finally realized that when I led that way, I was restricting followers in using their gifts because they all were not wired to operate like I was in that capacity. My lack of self-control (Prov 25:28) was hurting the group. When

I realized that I was hindering their ministry, I changed. I established written rules concerning how many days out I would have all assignments in team members' hands. By supplying weekly reminders and to-do tasks, I provided all team members at least ten days of sufficient leeway time to prepare to bring their best. As a result of my discipline, I noticed an incredible shift in their quality of work.

3. **Thorough Content** - Depending upon how you get resources to your team will determine what you provide for them. While many teams will rely on printed materials and physical audio copies, a growing number of teams share content on online platforms. In these settings, the team leader can post online all of the needed sheet music, chord charts, lyric sheets, video clips, and audio recordings. Team members can practice in their home office, on the commute to work, or right from their phone. While you don't need to eliminate the option for creative flexibility when the team comes together, do as much as you can to provide thorough content when you send things to team members. If you aren't going to lead the song like the audio recording you are providing, explain the differences. If you are transposing the key for the band, transpose what they are listening to so they can practice within the expected range. The more thorough you can deliver your content, the more thorough the team can prepare for rehearsal. While these things may seem relatively small, your work done in a heartily manner is an offering to the Lord (Col 3:23).

The worship leader has his responsibilities, but the worship team does as well. The worship team should commit to:

1. **Critical Listening** - The manner in which a team member prepares for worship practice is immensely important. If members come to practice unfamiliar with the songs, the time together can easily get frustrating. As individuals, we are to make the best use of the time because the days are evil (Eph 5:16). If we fail to utilize our own time wisely, we run the risk of taking time away from others as well. Even if team members are listening to the music on the go, they can simply engage in passive listening. Passive listening leads to unprepared musicians, unprepared musicians lead to frustrating practices, and frustrating practices lead to distracted worship leading. The best way to get the most out of the group's rehearsal time is if members will individually engage in critical listening before practice. Critical listening means you are diagramming the song so that you grasp your individual part and how your contribution fits in as a part within the whole song. While I expect all members to employ this model, sometimes I can tell when everyone is not bringing adequate preparation to rehearsal. When the need arises, I incorporate a listening guide for a group to fill out utilizing critical listening. To take it even a step further, I will often play the song a second time and give each musician a different instrument for which to script the parts. What this step provides is a way for each of your group members to study and appreciate the roles of

the other musicians. It also provides an accountability opportunity for a band member to remind another that they don't need to be too busy at every single moment during a song.

2. **Focused Preparation** - After you have listened critically to the music and diagrammed your part, now is the time to work on your contribution. Multitasking will not be sufficient. A harvest doesn't come without preparation (Prov 6:8). If you commit to having a focused amount of preparation time, you will be able to come to rehearsal primed and ready to go. For instrumentalists, play along with the music or a click track to lock in timing. For vocalists, record yourself singing and notice areas for improvement. The goal of this focused preparation time is to practice the repertoire so much that the rehearsal time and worship leading time does not keep you anxious about the troublesome transitions. Work the details out in your personal preparation in order that you can be relaxed when you gather with the rest of the team. Make your parts feel comfortable so that you can focus on leading others in worship rather than worrying about missing a note.

3. **Selfless Attitude** - As you prepare, remember that we are called to imitate Jesus who humbled himself (Phil 2:5-8). In fact, we are called to put others needs above our own needs (Phil 2:3-4). To do that, prepare in a way that allows you to serve other team members. As you look through other members' assignments, can you rejoice over how each one will be used or are you

questioning why you weren't asked to cover a particular part? Can you look forward with anticipation to their offerings or just judge with degradation concerning the lack of your opportunities? Before you come, pray for the other team members. When you arrive at practice, encourage the rest of the team In reality, the greatest way you can support other team members is by practicing well before coming to rehearsal. Your preparation allows you freedom to serve them as they work on their parts. While your leader isn't perfect, remember that God has placed that leader over your team. As you submit to the leader's direction, realize that he has to give an account for how he watched over you. "Let them do this with joy and not with groaning, for that would be of no advantage to you" (Heb 13:17).

Group Rehearsal

If the team prepares before practice, group rehearsal will go so much smoother. Having prepared team members does not guarantee a successful practice. Even with prepared individuals, without a thoughtful game plan from the leader and without a dedicated mindset from the team members, practice could still become stressful for everyone. In order to have a successful worship team practice, both the team leader and the team members should commit to certain things.

The worship leader should commit to:

1. **Spiritual Preparation** - Regardless of when you have scheduled rehearsal, you are gathering together a group of people who have all lived a lot of life that particular day. As the team assembles, each member brings in a collection of stressful situations related to job, family, and health issues. Jumping into practice without providing a space to pause could be detrimental to the entire rehearsal. In an attempt to be time sensitive, I used to think that I didn't have the margin to do any type of spiritual development for the team. After years of rehearsing groups, I have realized that it is detrimental to the group's health if I neglect this critical aspect. This daily encouragement fights against the team from being hardened by sin (Heb 3:13). I have found that fifteen minutes of spiritual development actually shortens the practice rather than lengthens it. I can imagine the math seems off in your mind, but that investment in obtaining focus pays off incredible dividends. Regardless of who is present, I always start rehearsal on time with a period of spiritual development for whoever is there. All it takes is a concentrated time in the Word and a time to pray for one another. After those brief minutes, everyone seems more calm and connected, and practice goes great. Plus the ones who are consistently late realize that we aren't going to wait on them and start gradually arriving earlier.

2. **Productive Order** - As the leader, make sure that you are cognizant of how challenging the musical collection is per week. If you do all new or newer songs, anticipate a long rehearsal. If you do a few

challenging pieces, anticipate a frustrating rehearsal. As you plan, make sure that the entirety of the music can be mastered in one week's rehearsal. In addition, make sure that you have a productive order for practice. After a time of spiritual preparation, proceed in an order that is both encouraging and intentional. It is wise to start and end on music that will be more familiar. By starting with a familiar song, everyone gets into rhythm with one another. As everyone starts hitting a stride, introduce the newer or more challenging music. By this point, everyone should be more limber and comfortable, and the sound issues should have been worked out by that point. If at all possible, end rehearsal on a song that will cause everyone to leave feeling encouraged. If you start and end practice well, the group will most likely walk away excited about the opportunity to lead at the upcoming gathering.

3. **Clear Communication** - One of the greatest challenges of the team leader is how to clearly communicate with all the team members especially because each person learns in different types of ways. Just as we are meant to study one another in order to serve as a positive catalyst in others' lives (Heb 10:24), the team leader must realize that different people require different types of communication to promote excellence on the team. Your classically-trained musicians are going to require a certain type of direction, and your by-the-ear musicians require something completely different altogether. In addition, you have auditory, visual, and kinesthetic

learners on your team who all benefit from differing types of instruction. Learn your team members and clearly communicate with each of them. Make sure that if information needs to be shared with everyone that you first get everyone's attention if they are distracted with side conversations and instrumental doodling. State your expectations clearly and then give a few opportunities to attempt them.

In addition to the worship leader's responsibilities for rehearsal, the worship team should commit to:

1. **Timely Arrival** - If practice starts at 6:00, that does not mean start setting your guitar rig up at 6:00. When you are late to rehearsal, it not only causes you to spend more time there, but it also forces everyone else to alter their schedules to accommodate your inconsiderate tardiness. King Solomon instructed us to watch the ants at how wisely they stay focused at the task at hand (Prov 6:6). Plan your day accordingly and get to rehearsal before it begins. Calculate how long it will take to have everything situated and be ready to follow the leader at the designated time with everything ready to go. It should be embarrassing to keep everyone waiting, so work hard and don't let it happen anymore.

2. **Considerate Participation** - When it is time to begin a song, be ready to do your part. When it is time to pause a song and communicate, be considerate of everyone's time and nerves and stop messing around. You are a part of this worship team because you love music, and so does everyone else in the group. If you

take everyone's time by continually practicing when the leader is trying to communicate, it shows disrespect for the leader and for everyone else's time. If you have prepared well before rehearsal, you shouldn't need the breaks to work on something – you have already mastered it by this point. Your practice in rehearsal reveals to the group you are unprepared. By continuing to be busy when the leader is trying to communicate with everyone, you reveal that you weren't ready for rehearsal and that you don't value the dynamic of the group.

3. **Thorough Note-Taking** - Take detailed notes during practice so that you don't forget anything you need to work on specifically. Every group knows the pain of rehearsing that difficult transition numerous times only to have someone forget it when you reconvene a few days later. While each of us will have mental or physical slips from time to time, it shouldn't be a regular issue. If you require music in front of you as you lead, then you should be able to take specific notes from your leader and from your mistakes in practice that should alert you of any impending challenge when you near it in the song. Whether you take notes best on paper or electronically, commit to take specific annotations. When you get home and have a chance for last preparations before the worship gathering, take out those notes and work on the troubled spots. Remove any anxiety from your leading so that you are free to actually worship rather than worry.

Corporate Worship

After individual preparation and group practice, we finally arrive at the time to lead worship in our corporate gatherings. Don't allow your unpreparedness to rob you from these moments! A worship service is not a performance for people, but it is a time when we offer our worship to God and try to encourage others to join along with us.

During this time, all worship team members are responsible to:

1. **Execute Skillfully** - If each member has prepared well, and the entire team has practiced well, the worship gathering shouldn't be a stressful time for the worship team. Everyone has experienced the nerves associated with nearing the more difficult moment in a song. If everyone has done their work before the gathering, stress should have been eliminated by this point. In a worship gathering, no matter how hard you practice, it won't be a perfect offering. In your area of control, stay focused on your offering and lead with your absolute best. The congregation has brought plenty of distractions with them into worship, don't add any to them by failing to be prepared and offer your best (Ps 33:3).

2. **Express Passionately** - As you lead others in worship, show them that you mean what you say. People in worship don't necessarily have to believe what the leaders believe, but they should believe that the leaders believe it. Don't manufacture fake expressions

or meaningless presentations with no authenticity behind them. Never believe that the most flamboyant expressions are the most sincere ones either. I have been led in more sincere worship by the humble than by the rowdy. Don't try to be someone you are not. If God made you meek and mild, lead from your humble spirit. If God made you bold and rowdy, lead from your passionate spirit. Being authentic is a greater trait than being manufactured. In your passionate yet real expressions, you set the bar for the rest of the congregation. Rarely will a congregation surpass the passion of the team leading. The worship team sets the standard for the congregation concerning engagement, involvement, and passion.

3. **Maintain Professionally** - Mistakes will happen. Your team will cringe over more blunders than the congregation will ever notice, but if and when they happen, don't acknowledge that they happened. If something goes wrong, don't let your face show it. Don't all turn around and grimace at the one who made the error. Don't stop for it, don't talk about it, don't frown about it, but just continue offering leadership for the good of the service. As a worship team, you are trying to change the paradigm that causes so many congregants to believe that you are the performers and they are the audience. Once you remove the fear of man from your life in the first place, you are able to remember that you are leading for the approval of God and never for a person (Gal 1:10).

Great is the LORD, and greatly should he be praised (Ps 48:1; 96:4; 145:3). Don't give unworthy offerings to one so worthy. Why? Because he knows your heart. He really knows your heart. Will you be willing to do the hard work in order to offer him your absolute best?

4. DETACHMENT

Bear one another's burdens, and so fulfill the law of Christ (Gal 6:2).

The fourth worship team killer is detachment. While pride and inconsistency are internal dangers, inability the external danger, detachment is a relational danger. Detachment can kill a worship team when they isolate themselves from the rest of the congregation. Not only will detachment kill the dynamic of the worship team, but it will also kill the effectiveness of the worship team concerning their impact upon the congregation.

You will have minimal impact where you have minimal presence.

I learned this reality firsthand when I transitioned into the role of Worship Pastor while our church was in the middle of a worship center construction. I suddenly became invited to numerous meetings with architects, designers, and engineers. Coming into the discussions late into the process, I often had questions or suggestions regarding the future of that local church and how it related to the current building project.

One building concept was a strange addition to the plan. The unique plan included a church green room. I had always thought of a green room as a place where the entertainers were protected from the audience in order to provide the best performance possible. So, why would a church even need a green room?

- The worship team is not a group of **entertainers**.
- Those in attendance are not the **audience**.
- The goal of worship should not be **performance**.

I was honestly unsure of what benefit a green room would create for our congregation. I was told by architectural experts that many churches our size had a green room where the pastor and the band could prepare and unplug while it wasn't their specific time to be leading on stage. While I didn't buy into all the intricacies of the concept, I did understand the need concerning having a set place to gather, discuss, and pray before the service. Since the space was available and had a somewhat logical intended purpose, I didn't make too big a deal about it.

Once we opened the worship center, my reactions taught me something. Anytime anyone would speak on stage or off stage regarding a meeting happening in the green room, I would cringe. The phrase literally made me sick to my stomach. A green room implied that there was some type of separation between the leaders and the congregants. It implied that an elite group needed to be protected from such distractions as real people with real needs. It made me feel like we were there just to perform a task on a stage devoid of relationships with people. If it appears I made too big a deal about this, you must realize that I am fiercely opposed to inheriting the behaviors of the world within the church.

It is always a tragedy when the people of God learn how to worship God from those who do not know God.

The Bible warns about learning worship practices from the world.

- God would not allow Nadab and Abihu to offer "strange fire" upon the altar because it was a practice discouraged in Scripture (Lev 10:1).

- God was angry enough to kill Uzzah (2 Sam 6:7) when he cared for the things of God in the same manner which he learned from the pagan Philistines (1 Sam 6:8).

- Jesus would quote Isaiah (Isa 29:13) by warning against worshipping according to what we learn from man rather than what is commanded by God (Mark 7:7).

While the concept of a green room is not as severe as those examples mentioned, it is a symptom of a larger problem – the Church is often too prone to adopt the principles of this world than we are to obey the commands of Scripture. We tend to take our cues from the world and try to apply them directly within our churches. Any attempt to baptize worldly practices can never truly convert sinful motivations. It doesn't matter how musicians operate in the world. The world's standard should never dictate the church's mission.

There is no room for celebrities in our churches.

Unfortunately, worship teams are becoming more and more detached from the congregations they are called to serve. While I prefer not having a green room, I don't fault churches who do. There are practical benefits to the inclusion but the subtle consequences should be considered. If you do see the need for a green room, I encourage you to make time to be around the people in your church during gathering times.

Whether or not there is a green room locality, many worship teams possess a green room mentality. Viewing themselves as the musical nobility within the congregation, they only associate with each other, ignore other members, and remove themselves from the possibility of learning anything during a service.

While I believe it to be advantageous for any worship team to be focused on the task at hand, I think we may have picked up some wrong tasks along the way. If our worship leading doesn't involve us uniting with the people in the congregation in a relational way, I believe we have missed the reasoning for the worship gatherings. If the worship team is only supposed to churn out people's favorite worship anthems, the original artists have better versions to which you could listen to at home.

Something unique happens when the people of God gather together and we must commit to pursuing that.

Detachment changes our priorities. We begin to fixate on the programs rather than the people. While I want our entire team to lead in an exemplary fashion, am I willing to divorce them from the people they serve in order to implement an impeccable service?

I would prefer a band member to be late on stage because he or she was ministering to someone than the whole team locked away in isolation from the rest of the church. We can churn out everyone's favorite worship songs like you hear them on the radio and yet lose our effectiveness because we are not engaged with those we are leading. Prepared and polished are not the only goals of our worship. We want to do things in a spirit of excellence (Ps 33:3), but we must desire to have solid relationships with people even more (Gal 6:10).

Ministering to people off the stage allows me to be a more effective minister when I am on the stage. I don't want to lead the church based off the world's wisdom when I have the Word's truth in front of me:

1. Sharing my life with the local church should come from a place of genuine love for the people (1 Thess 2:8).
2. As a pastor, I am called to be hospitable in my home and in the church house (1 Tim 3:3).

3. I want to be able to teach both in public and in homes (Acts 20:20) showing that relationships should be built in each of those environments.

4. I want to embrace this priesthood of believers (1 Pet 2:9) and realize that all of those gathered have something given by the Spirit for the edification of the whole body (Eph 4:12; Rom 12:5; 1 Cor 12:7, 27).

5. I want to fight against an air of spiritual superiority (1 Cor 4:7) and acknowledge that no one is more important than another (Gal 6:3).

6. I want to be physically present with this church and have all things in common with them (Acts 2:44).

7. I want Jesus' prayer over us to be true – that we would be one (John 17:21).

8. I want the incredible privilege and responsibility of bearing one another's burdens and thereby fulfilling the law of Christ (Gal 6:2).

I am not a fan of the church green room because there is no room for celebrities among us. How can we detach ourselves from the people we are called to lead? If we examine our practices, we will often be able to discern our hearts. Let us lead with the wisdom of the Word rather than the practices of the world.

Reasons for Detachment

The fact that detachment is detrimental to worship ministry is obvious, but the reason why people detach can differ.

1. **Elitism** - Some people detach due to elitism. They think they are simply better than others. Our American Church culture bucks against the priesthood of the believer (1 Pet 2:9) and embraces creating a Christian celebrity culture. Even the early Corinthian church struggled with flocking to their favorite leaders (1 Cor 3:4-5). Paul had to remind them that elite leaders do not exist because God is the only one truly capable of causing spiritual growth within a church (1 Cor 3:7). From the Corinthian churches to the current churches, we have created spiritual hierarchies and judged people based on external qualities which reveals our wicked thoughts (James 2:4). It does not help us that our stages are elevated, our faces are projected, our spaces are separated, and our talents are highlighted. Even the best of motivations can start to buy what our church consumeristic culture is selling.

2. **Favoritism** - Some worship leaders are detached from their congregations due to favoritism. While we would like to appear as if cliques were absent from the church, they can often run rampant. While it is normal and biblical to have a few close friends (Prov 18:24), it is selfish and sinful to avoid people who aren't in your inner circle. Naturally,

you are going to spend a significant portion of time with other worship team members due to the time commitment involved. In order to combat any tinge of favoritism, what are you willing to do to befriend those in your congregation who would never be on the stage? The Pharisees in Jesus' day had a reputation for creating a culture of favoritism among the people of God. They loved to be recognized and would only sit in the places of honor with other people of honor (Matt 23:5-7). Jesus claimed that their attitudes shut the kingdom of heaven in people's faces (Matt 23:13) as they would ignore the needs of the endangered (Luke 10:31-32), avoid the gatherings of the sinners (Matt 9:11), and refuse to deal with those ethnically different than them (John 4:9). Jesus was opposed to favoritism and was even criticized due to the type of people he befriended (Mark 2:16-17). We are not to be haughty but associate with all types of people (Rom 12:16).

3. **Individualism** - Elitism makes you snobbish, favoritism makes you cliquish, and individualism makes you standoffish. Individualism will detach you from the congregation either because you simply don't trust people or don't believe that you need people. All of us have trust issues stemming from those who have hurt us in the past. To combat that trend in our lives, bitterness must be put away and forgiveness must be embraced (Eph 4:31-32). Don't give someone in your past the authority to ruin your relationships in the future.

On the other hand, if you believe that you don't need others, you are in the most dangerous position possible. You do need other believers in your life (Heb 3:13; 10:25), but let's just postulate that you didn't need others in your life (which I think is absolutely ludicrous), have you ever considered that maybe someone else needs you in his or her life? If you are *that* put together, how much could you benefit others! How could someone of your maturity neglect the rest of us who are still broken and needy? If you have arrived, we need your directions more than you can imagine. Truthfully, you do need others, but you must realize that Christian community is not only about what you get out of it but what you put into it.

Platform ministry can never replace relational ministry.

Regardless of why you detach, you must acknowledge the danger of an indifferent attitude towards Christian community. When people are gifted in the arts, they are often put on a stage to perform a certain type of ministry. While time on the stage may be an outlet for ministry, oftentimes, the time off the stage substantiates the ministry. Someone can sing in your church and raise the rafters with their vocal pipes. The song can provide an emotional experience overflowing with goosebumps, but it cannot compare with a talented worship leader who is intimately involved in the lives of the people in the church.

While time on stage may provide ministry affirmation, the time off stage provides ministry validation.

The more involved your worship team is in the life of the church aside from stage time makes your ministry so much more effective. If those leading in song are also leading in life, the congregation will follow them anywhere. Credibility is earned and not given.

Every church experiences conflict concerning worship preferences. When changes are made, people do not hesitate to share their passionate opinions. When a worship team stays connected to the body, they will have greater success in leading any needed change. I believe that some changes take place in churches with minimal conflict because the members may not trust the direction, but they do trust the ones leading. If you want to accomplish more than acquiring a standing ovation, you are going to have to war against detachment from your congregation.

Availability - Leading with Presence

The solution to detachment is availability. Worship leaders must learn how to lead with presence. It does your church a disservice if you lead from a distance. Every worship team member must make it a priority to be incarnational in their ministry. To impact people, you must be among the people.

Jesus had compassion on the people because "they were harassed and helpless, like sheep without a shepherd" (Matt 9:36). To be a shepherd, you must be around sheep! What did Jesus do to help all of these stressed sheep that he saw? He prayed for more workers to come into the harvest who would shepherd these people (Matt 9:38). If you are in church leadership, guess what? He prayed for you!

Jesus never prays for more skillful people, but he does pray for more shepherd-like people. He prays that shepherds would surround the sheep. He still lives to make intercession (Heb 7:25) for that type of leaders. Oh, what grace! Oh, what joyous wonder to behold! The King of kings prays for you and me!

He might pray for us what he prayed for Peter that his faith would not fail (Luke 22:32). Maybe he prays that we would be sanctified by the word of truth (John 17:17). Maybe he prays that we live not by our wills but by God's will (Luke 22:42). Nearing the cross, Jesus prayed for himself, his disciples, and also future believers like us. In that prayer, he prayed for our unity (John 17:21).

Jesus prayed that we would not be detached from one another but that we would be present with one another.

By being available to your church family, you are actually becoming the answer to Jesus' prayers!

Up Close and Personal

While I have been a participant in many memorable moments of worship, some instances stand out above the rest. The most unforgettable moments of worship are usually those with more meaning than more flash. The hymn had never been so powerful for our church than when a mother who had recently buried her young son honestly poured her heart over the lines: "whatever my lot, thou has taught me to say, 'it is well, it is well with my soul." When the singer led our church in singing, "in the good times and bad, you are on your throne, you are God alone," right after the singer's spouse had been diagnosed with cancer, faith was swelling up in that place. When the disabled, elderly saint belted out, "when I die, hallelujah, by and by, I'll fly away," a great truth carried an even greater weight.

No amount of skill can accomplish what accessibility provides. When you know your congregation and your congregation knows you, there is something deeper transpiring than just musical selections. The separation between the leaders and the congregants fades. No longer are we seeing a worship team as performers and viewing the worshipers as spectators. When a worship team exemplifies availability, the gathering becomes more of a family than an audience. Worship becomes a time for the family to circle up together in order to thank their Father for how good he has been. Someone picks the songs and gets them going, but in those moments, it ceases to be a spectator event.

Worship leaders, work on the time you lead on the stage, but spend even more time on the way you lead off the stage.

Worship teams are limited in their effectiveness if they lead from a distance. It should be a priority of a worship team to be involved in the life of a church and not just the activity on a stage. If we are not in the lives of those worshiping with us, we lose touch with the rest of the

Body of Christ and can risk just performing songs for people. To be truly available, the following is necessary:

1. **Church Member** - In order to participate as a regular, team members should be church members for the sake of accountability and discipline (Heb 10:25; Acts 2:42; 20:28; Rom. 12:4-5). Some people might want to be a part of your musical team but not be a part of your church family. That person is wanting benefits with no responsibility. They want notoriety without accountability. Someone desiring to serve on a worship team should first commit to the church, and then after an adequate amount of time being a member, which allows church leaders to gauge commitment level (Heb 13:17), he or she should be considered for the ministry. If needed, a letter of recommendation from the pastor or worship leader of a previous church would be beneficial in getting to know the commitment level of a new worship team member. It would also provide insight into why this person left the previous church and the manner in which this person left. This type of interaction might reveal if the prospective team member is a fair-weathered church hopper who is looking for the next gig or a mature person who wants to commit to this particular expression of the local church.

2. **Connected with Other Believers** - It is more important for a Christian to be involved in discipleship relationships than it is to serve on a ministry team. If you only have time for one, you need to be committed to a group of believers intent on developing your faith.

Whether it is a discipleship group, a class, a group of committed friends, or an accountability partner, you need to be involved in some type of Christian community. It is possible that a ministry team can function as both but it must be an intentional commitment. In Christian community, we sharpen one another (Prov 27:17), encourage one another (1 Thess 5:11), confront one another (Matt 18:15-20), speak truth to one another (Eph 4:15), confess sins to one another (Jam 5:16) and fellowship with one another (Acts 2:42). If the goal is that we mature in Christ completely (Col 1:28), we must commit to engage with one of the most pivotal tools God gives us to accomplish this task – each other.

3. **Ministry Support** - Demonstration of Christian values and beliefs should be shown on and off the stage, whether through participation on a worship team or support of another ministry group. Since worship teams are displayed on stages, they must work hard to indicate that they value other ministry teams that don't have such a visible platform. Every ministry team and every church member is important to the building up of the Body of Christ (Eph 4:16; 1 Cor 12:27). Many team members won't have sufficient time to join another group, but you can pray for other ministries, write encouraging notes to other teams, and brag on other teams in front of people. Ministry is difficult and encouraging other ministry teams is a good work (Gal 6:10) that will soften the hardening that often happens due to the deceitfulness of sin (Heb 3:13).

4. **Service Attendance** - Worship teams need to be present in worship services. While this may seem like a given, it is progressively becoming a decreasing reality. If you aren't on the schedule for a worship service, that doesn't mean you should skip the worship service. If you aren't on the stage in a worship service, that doesn't mean you should leave the worship service. We never want to give anyone the idea that we are too good to sit in a service in which we are not leading on that day or at that moment. In particular, I believe it is very advantageous to the soul of the worship leader and the morale of the congregation for the worship team to be visibly present during sermons. If you have multiple services, I don't believe it is necessary to sit in all services, but it is important to sit in at least one. Hearing biblical preaching sanctifies us in the Word (John 17:17), establishes sound doctrine (Titus 2:1), washes our souls (John 15:3; Eph. 5:26), and trains us for godliness by equipping us for every good work (2 Tim 3:16-17). Even if you are perfect, one more sermon isn't going to hurt you.

To Be Available Like Jesus

All of the above components have one goal in mind – being available to minister to those in need. There is no greater role model than Jesus himself. Not only did he leave heaven to take on flesh for our sake (John 1:14) at just the right time (Gal 4:4), he became poor (2 Cor 8:9), weak (2 Cor 13:4), and similar to us (Heb 2:17) in order that he could condemn sin in the flesh (Rom. 8:3). He became available to us so that he could sympathize with our weaknesses (Heb 4:15) in order that he could come to our side for assistance in temptation (Heb 2:18).

Even when Jesus was sorrowful and stressed, he made himself available to others. When Jesus had just learned that his forerunner and cousin, John the Baptist, had just been executed, he sought solitude in order to mourn (Matt 14:13). Just like many of us, he was suffering with a loss and desired to be alone. He was probably attempting to get a chance to withdraw in order to pray to his Father alone as was his custom (Mark 1:35; Luke 6:12; 22:39).

Seeking this solitude, he was interrupted by those who needed him. What is remarkable about Jesus is not only what he did but what he didn't do.

Jesus never dismissed the needs of others in order to care for his own needs.

Jesus had compassion on them (Matt 14:14). They were sick. They needed help, and he committed to assist them all day even until sunset. Even when the disciples urged him to send the people away, Jesus pointed to their need and told the disciples not to hand it off to another but to handle it themselves (Matt 14:16). Jesus never used an entourage, a barrier, or an excuse to protect him from the people he came to save.

People needed Jesus more than Jesus needed solitude.

More than just this example, Jesus' life is characterized by his unwillingness to detach from people even when he was weary. Jesus left the disciples to pray one morning and they found him anyway (Mark 1:35-26). He was unable to enter anywhere and remain unnoticed (Mark 1:45). Even when Jesus would withdraw, people would bring their sick to him (Luke 5:15-17). Whether he would withdraw to a beach (Mark 2:13), a lake (Mark 6:31), or a field (Mark 2:23), the crowd would always locate him. He would notice when a needy woman would reach out for him (Luke 8:45) and refused to send those precious children, whom the disciples saw as pesky, away from his presence (Matt 19:14).

I do see that Jesus taught the importance of occasional solitude, but I can't get past the fact that the needs of others always surpassed his own. Jesus never let isolation get in the way of ministry. His example in ministry greatly challenges my desire to be an isolated Christian who keeps the door closed and the people out.

Since Jesus did not come to be served but to serve (Mark 10:45), Jesus had an uncanny knack of identifying with people and empathizing with them regarding their needs. Jesus was able to ascertain current events and evaluate how to minister to people's true spiritual needs. Due to his close proximity to people, he was able to identify with them on a personal level.

Not regarding equality with God as something to be grasped (Phil 2:6), the Creator and Savior of the world identified with his creation so much that he would even ask, "What do you want me to do for you?" (Mark 10:36). Jesus displayed a leader who was not too great to hear the petitions of his followers. While Jesus did not grant every request made by his disciples (Mark 10:38-40), his willingness to listen to them gained trust in his followers that many other leaders never actually acquire.

As Christ dwelt among the people of this earth (John 1:14), he was able to identify with their pain and struggles. Jesus led in such an empathetic manner, that his disciples trusted his leadership and were eager to follow him. Jesus taught leaders that the sought positions should not be the places of prominence but among the broken people who are in need of a guide (Matt 23:9-12).

There is a price tag associated in identifying with people, and Jesus never had a problem paying for it.

Sincere commitment is reciprocal. When a leader commits to being available to the followers, the followers commit to being available to the leader.

Just think about this fact – Jesus was almost always with people. When Jesus called his twelve disciples, their initial primary objective was that they "might be with him" (Mark 3:14). They saw him on and off the ministry stage and had such rich memories that their stories could fill up enough books to overflow the whole world with all that he said and did of which we aren't even aware (John 21:25). How do they have these memories and the rest of the world doesn't know about them? Because they were close enough to him.

As a worship leader, you are guiding sheep through an important aspect within the church. Since ministry involves people, shepherding implies that you will be around the sheep. I can tend to be so busy with programs that I miss the people. Instead of rushing people off so I can get to my agenda, maybe I need to remember that they are my agenda. In an attempt to serve in worship ministry, I pray that you will never avoid the people to whom God is calling you to lead.

5. DIVISION

Behold, how good and pleasant it is when brothers dwell in unity (Ps 133:1).

If we don't allow our pride, inconsistency, inability, or detachment to kill our worship team, there is one final killer that will be happy to handle the assassination – division. Pride and inconsistency are the internal killers, inability is the external killer, and detachment and division are the relational killers. Detachment and division differ in the sense that detachment hinders your relationship with church members and division hinders your relationship with team members. Division will kill a worship team's ministry when they cease to display how to get along with each other.

As was previously noted, worship teams have spiritual targets on their backs. If your team has a desire to have a significant spiritual impact through the worship ministry in your specific context, the devilish squadrons will have you on their sinister radar. Prowling around like a predator, the devil seeks to destroy your team (1 Pet 5:8). One of the primary ways he will seek to accomplish this task will be through enlisting people around you to frustrate the Kingdom work (2 Tim 2:26). While we acknowledge that persecution comes along with the territory of any Christian's attempt at godliness (2 Tim 3:12), we must realize that Satan will use accusations from non-believers (1 Pet 2:12), opposition from church members (Rom 16:17; 2 Tim 2:25), and conflict from team members (1 Cor 1:10-13; 3:3; 11:18) to get the job done.

In spiritual warfare, we are exhorted to put on the full armor of God in order to stand against the schemes of the devil (Eph 6:11). As you diagram the pieces of armor that the Apostle Paul describes, you realize the one area that is not covered is the backside.

The armor of God doesn't include backside armor because we were never meant to run from a spiritual attack and we should never have to worry about being stabbed in the back from a fellow soldier.

Wouldn't that be grand if it were the case? As the Body of Christ, we are meant to cover each other's backs from spiritual attacks and not look for exposed places and opportune times to do the job ourselves. Looking for opportune times to attack is the schematic plans of the devil (Luke 4:13; Eph 4:27) and should not be a part of the arsenal plan of the believer towards a brother or sister in Christ. Instead of watching over one another's back, we are often found stabbing one another in the back and known for the only type of group in the world that attacks their own wounded.

Beta Fish Syndrome

It is apparent when a worship team detaches from the rest of the congregation, but it can be less obvious when they distance themselves from one another. Both scenarios are dangerous. Stereotypically, artistic people can tend to suffer from beta fish syndrome. Beta fish are those beautiful, flamboyant fish that are very mesmerizing to watch. In fact, as you observe beta fish, they appear to be very docile and tranquil aquatic pets.

That is until you put them in a tank with another beta fish. These seemingly peaceful animals turn into bloodthirsty assassins who will not rest until the other fish is decimated. I'm not even sure how these fish murder each other, but they will not stop until one buoys up to the top of the fish bowl and the other swims away victorious.

You are on a worship team because you have some level of prominence about you. Something within your skill set causes others to stand outside the bowl and marvel at what they see inside. Just like those beta fish, we can function well isolated but oftentimes cause issues when having to learn how to navigate the waters beside another like us. We function well when we are left alone, but we become unsettled when we have to work together.

As a member of a worship team, we must remember that we are a part of the Body of Christ, and we must learn how to put others' desires above our own (Phil. 2:3-4). If you stumbled upon a man on the side of the road with his hands grasping his own neck intently trying to choke the life out of himself, you would be confused and alarmed. How could someone use his own body part to hinder the body as a whole?

As a member of the Body of Christ, why would you utilize your part to endanger the life of the whole?

When we prioritize the comfort of our role over the health of our group, we have turned into the assassin ourselves. Once I make it about me over you, we have a problem. Disagreements will happen. Conflicts are unavoidable. You can't have people assembled without them. Acknowledging the inevitability of discord, is your team willing to address them biblically when it surfaces?

It makes no sense to worship our Father while we tear down his children (1 John 4:19-20). Any parent finds great delight when his or her children get along, how much more so with our Father in heaven? As a Father, God takes very personally any attack on any one of his children, and yet we lead in his name while attacking those who belong to him.

Reasons for Division

You might be aware that division exists on your worship team, but you may have never thought through why it exists. While there are many possible grounds why division might be present on your worship team, there are some common reasons that are seen frequently:

1. **Immature Members** - Some of the division on your team is that you have spiritually immature members. Physically, your average age may be 40 years old, but spiritually, the team members act like they are 4 years old. Part of Christian discipleship is maturing (Eph 4:13-14) and leaving childish ways behind (1 Cor 13:11). Where Christian maturity is lacking, division is guaranteed.

2. **Personality Differences** - Sometimes conflict happens simply because people are wired differently. Division can happen not because people are against one another but because they are simply not like one another. Your extroverts unnerve your introverts. Your touchy feely type fluster the personal space advocates. Some conflicts will have to be avoided by learning how to deal with the unchangeable and harmless differences present on your team.

3. **Hostile Personalities** - Division can often happen on a worship team simply due to the involvement of a divisive person. Unprovoked and unwarranted, some people are just down right hot-tempered who stir up strife wherever they go (Prov 15:18). There are those who claim the name of Christ and excel at devouring one another (Gal 5:15). By provoking people constantly (Gal 5:26), a

hostile person can set the whole thing on fire (Prov 16:27).

4. **Unresolved Issues** - Some teams can't get traction today or plan for tomorrow because baggage is still lying around from yesterday. Maybe the catalyst that caused the conflict in the past isn't happening anymore, but what was done back there was never addressed in a healthy manner. Without a pursuit of reconciliation (Heb 12:14), peace cannot exist where there has been conflict because no attempt is made (Rom 12:18).

5. **Disrespectful Attitudes** - If your team has disrespectful attitudes towards one another, they might fail to acknowledge or appreciate the contributions of other team members. In that type of environment, no one can celebrate the gifts of another because his or her gifts are not the ones being celebrated at that moment. If members aren't dedicated to loving one another (1 Thess 4:9) and promoting harmony (Rom 12:16), true unity will be hard to actualize.

6. **Warring Sects** - Beware of the meetings after the meetings. While worship teams can vary in size, smaller groups of people can form cliques and cause disunity among the ranks. Those who whisper and stir things up separate close friends and cause strife among the group (Prov 16:28). Those people who enjoy starting strife opens up the floodgates towards unthinkable and unnecessary issues (Prov 17:14).

7. **Unshared Vision** - One of the major ways teams divide is due to the lack of shared vision. The goal of being united in the same mind is critical (Phil 2:2; 1 Cor 1:10). If the oxen have to plow connected to one another, one cannot go left and the other go right. There must be a common and shared focus to accomplish unity. While each team member will have a different role, it is important that each team member be running in the same direction and at the same pace.

The Responsibility to Address Division

Every church struggles with discord at some level. Paul wrote to the Corinthians "that there be no divisions among you, but that you be united in the same mind and the same judgment" (1 Cor 1:10). When this church would come together, they experienced the antithesis of what should happen. They actually were worse gathered than when they were scattered (1 Cor 11:17). Gathering as the church, they each congregated within their own separate factions (1 Cor 11:18). These antagonistic groups were tangible evidence of the works of the flesh in their lives (Gal 5:20) rather than the peaceful evidence of the fruit of the Spirit (Gal 5:22).

When division exists in the church, God makes no allowance for indifference.

Whether you are the victim or the assailant, God holds you responsible for making it right. If you caused the division, he expects you to handle it. If you are the recipient of the division, he expects you to take the initiation to fix it.

While you can't ensure peace, you can do everything in your power to try to experience peace with another (Rom 12:18). Peace among the family of God is so important that it should be pursued rather than just hoping that it will happen on its own. We are called to bear with one another and to apply the amount of forgiveness to one another that we have received from Jesus himself (Col 3:13)! If it is your fault, seek forgiveness (James 5:16). If it isn't your fault, offer forgiveness (Matt 5:23-24). Either way, you take the initiative!

Every worshiper and worship leader enters into worship with distractions. One distraction that Jesus wants to ensure that you don't bring with you is tension with another worshiper. In the Sermon on the Mount, Jesus said, "Therefore, if you are offering your gift at the altar and there remember that your brother has something against you, leave your gift there in front of the altar. First go and be reconciled to your brother; then come and offer your gift" (Matt 5:23-24).

Many church members are familiar enough with this verse to misunderstand it. Jesus doesn't teach you to leave your offering of worship if you have something against your brother. You are to stop worshiping if you remember that your brother has something against you. If you understand that someone has something against you, you are still responsible to address it! Jesus doesn't cut us any slack.

If you are the wronger or the wronged, it is your responsibility to make it right.

It's normal to think that we should address our own bitterness, but we are also called to take the initiative regarding someone else's bitterness. Jesus excels in paradigm shifts. If you are merely aware that someone doesn't like you, fix it. If you acknowledge that someone has problems with you, do whatever you can within your power to make peace eagerly (Eph 4:3). Jesus also commands that you do it right away. Even if you remember the tension when you were in the middle of a worship service, Jesus is more pleased for you to walk out of the service in order for you to take care of business.

Would God really desire for worship attendance to go down numerically in order to secure relational reconciliation? Absolutely, he does! Our worship hinges on his forgiveness. How can we rejoice greatly about God's forgiveness for us while neglecting to show that grace towards others?

God isn't merely honored when we worship him with songs, but he wants us to worship him with our lives. What if the most God-honoring thing you could do in the next worship service or worship practice was to leave it? What if you got out your phone, went across the platform, or walked across the church campus and did something as radical as fix what is broken? The ministry of your worship team is hindered if you allow division on your team and in your church to go unchallenged.

Unity - Leading with Selflessness

Unity among God's people glorifies God. When we gather together, we should gather together as if we were one man (Ezra 3:1). Christians are a "chosen race, a royal priesthood, a holy nation, a people for God's own possession, so that you may proclaim the excellencies of him who has called you out of darkness into his marvelous light; for you once were not a people, but now you are the people of God" (1 Pet 2:9-10). Paul encouraged the church to be "of the same mind, maintaining the same love, united in spirit, intent on one purpose. Do nothing from selfishness or empty conceit, but with humility of mind regard one another as more important than yourselves" (Phil 2:3-4).

As believers, we are called to live with one another "without grumbling or disputing" (Phil 2:14) and possess a genuine unity of mind (1 Pet 3:8). Loving one another "binds everything together in perfect harmony" (Col 3:14). Experiencing this type of rapport will not come easily, but it will take diligent work to preserve a biblical sense of unity (Eph 4:3).

The early church fleshed out what it meant to be a church that was united. These men and women were very different and yet "had all things in common" (Acts 2:44; 4:32). They benefited from a united *place* to gather (Acts 1;13: 2:1, 46), a united *prayer* to pray (Acts 1:14; 3:1), and a united *pursuit* to seek (Acts 2:42, 47; 4:33).

As a team, we all have areas where we may be strong as well as areas in which we need to learn more. Working together to be the best we can be for the sake of lifting up

Jesus is what honors him. Laboring together as a team to develop our skills is necessary to lead others in worship, but striving for unity in the way we treat and respect one another is just as important of a focus in our attempts to glorify God.

To develop and maintain unity, certain aspects are necessary:

1. **Addressing Conflict** - If there is a disagreement, team members should work it out with each other or have a third party present to help resolve the issue. Sometimes disagreements are just simple misunderstandings and should be treated as such. Having the opportunity to discuss what has transpired is the first step needed for reconciliation and the intentional aim should be nothing short of full restoration (2 Cor 13:11). Jesus taught us the proper progression of reconciliation by using three settings: private (Matt 18:15), partnership (Matt 18:16), and public (Matt 18:17). When addressing conflict, first approach the person in private. If that confrontation is unsuccessful, then bring along one or two others into the situation to be outside ears and voices. If that gathering cannot remedy the conflict, then the sin issue needs to be addressed in front of the church. Keep in mind that when Jesus said "church" in this moment, there was no formal church building in mind. The word *ekklesia* means "group" or "assembly." In the worship team context, if a sinful attitude is confronted in private and then addressed along with

some partners and the person is still unrepentant, then the group must get involved in some way.

2. **Implementing Discipline** - If someone is rude or consistently negative, this person needs to be addressed. If something is wrong, the leader should try and help address the need. If rudeness to other team members or church members continues, that person should be removed from leadership (2 Thess 3:14; Titus 1:13; 1 Cor 5:13). While this type of action seems countercultural in our church settings, it is because we have forgotten the necessity of leadership integrity. If you are pushing back because it sounds judgmental, you must realize that Jesus never taught to abstain from judgment – he warned against being a hypocrite while administering judgment (Matt 7:1-5). Judgment and discipline given in love is a good thing because it addresses the sin in my life (the log that Jesus spoke of) and it addresses the sin in your life (the speck that he spoke of). I don't want the reputation of Jesus marred due to my hypocrisy or your hypocrisy.

3. **Characterizing Selflessness** - Worship teams should never have to endure self-promoting divas. For those who are wanting to baptize a selfish desire for stage time in an encouraging environment such as the church, you need to find another place to perform. Those seeking a spotlight should not join the team. Put others before yourself (Phil 2:3-4) and treat others the way you would like to be treated (Matt 7:12).

4. **Prioritizing Servanthood** - Jesus gives us the penultimate example of servanthood in that he did

regard equality with God as something to be grasped but humbled himself for the benefit of others (Phil 2:5-8). One of the greatest ways to achieve unity is by serving other team members. A culture of servanthood is contagious and can be imitated by the entire congregation. Don't expect the leader, another member, or a church member to serve you. How can you serve those in your church family?

Biblical unity is the goal but this type of unity will not happen by accident. In fact, sometimes you have to cause more conflict now in order to experience more peace later. If there are people causing division, you will have to correct your opponents but correct them with a spirit of gentleness (2 Tim 2:25) in hopes that they will come to their senses and escape the will of the devil (2 Tim 2:26). As Christ would pray to keep us from the devil's schemes (John 17:15), is it any surprise that it was in the context of his prayer regarding our unity (John 17:11, 21, 22)?

If division is the devil's plan, we must war against his subterfuge. We cannot remain passive as we watch dissension rise among God's people. Failing to warn people about their quarreling words will only allow further conflict (2 Tim 2:14). At times, we must warn one another about wasting time and energy on foolish and ignorant controversies (2 Tim 2:23) and avoid them ourselves (Titus 3:8), but if there is genuine discord, we must address it.

If you are aware of continual disagreement, you might have to strongly urge warring factions to reconcile (Phil 4:2). Always be prepared to offer a loving rebuke when it seems necessary (2 Tim 4:2) but do it with authority (Titus

2:15). An open rebuke is always better than a hidden love (Prov 27:5). Rebuking a continually divisive person can also serve as a wakeup call for all people within the church (1 Tim 5:20) to acknowledge the serious nature of disunity. If the divisive person will not backdown, Scripture teaches that there is a time when you need to remove that individual from leadership and possibly even church fellowship (Titus 3:10). As we pray that the divisive person will return from his or her wandering (James 5:20), we are always ready to restore the repentant with a spirit of gentleness (Gal 6:1).

The Tuning Standard

Imagine that it is time to start Sunday morning soundcheck. As your entire worship team arrives, people are getting the essentials in place and begin to tune up their instruments. Instead of using any electronic regulated pitch, the bassist tunes his instrument by using the acoustic guitar which is a bit flat to begin with. The electric guitar then uses the bass to tune his guitar but his ears have trouble ascertaining the lower pitches. The entire team uses their ears one by one and tunes their instrument based off the imperfectly tuned instrument before them. When everyone says they are ready to go, you count off the timing to begin. As the first chord plays, your mouth is unable to describe what your ears are experiencing. The key is not established, and everything sounds close enough and yet far enough to be incredibly frustrating. Not only will the singers have a difficult time figuring out where to sing among this auditory conglomeration, the congregation will be completely lost.

What was the problem? They were trying to tune to each other rather than an outside standard. That's how most of us misunderstand the concept of unity. Pursuing unity is not bending to one another, but rather, it is bending together towards another standard.

In many orchestras, the oboist uses a modern electronic meter to ensure he or she is in tune, and then the bright, permeating sound of the oboe cascades over the entire orchestra as they all rally to that one pitch. They unify around something they know to be concrete. The entire performance that day is contingent upon each of them tuning to a standard higher than each individual instrument.

Unity will never be found by tuning to one another but by tuning to the standard-bearer.

Unity the Qualifier

With 150 psalms in Israel's hymnbook, it is easy to imagine that the majority of them focus on the object of our worship. While that is true to some extent, many of the psalms also describe the method of our worship or the character of our worship. Psalm 133 is a short psalm that describes an integral component of our worship more than it does the one we worship.

"Behold, how good and pleasant it is when brothers dwell in unity! It is like the precious oil on the head, running down on the beard, on the beard of Aaron, running down on the collar of his robes! It is like the dew of Hermon, which falls on the mountains of Zion! For there the LORD has commanded the blessing, life forevermore" (Ps 133:1-3).

I have always loved the first verse because I understood it. For years, I would neglect the reading and teaching of verses 2-3 because I honestly couldn't comprehend what the psalmist was talking about. What does unity have to do with oil dripping from a dead priest's beard and dew cascading from a mountain top? When I finally understood what these verses meant, the first verse and the concept of unity became all the more significant.

It is a very good and pleasant thing when God's people dwell together in unity (Ps 133:1). This type of unity is beneficial and agreeable to all. As the people of God unite, they compliment one another and yet were never intended to clone one another.

So how does Aaron fit in this picture of unity? Aaron served as the first high priest of Israel and started a succession of levitical priests that would come from his family (Ex 28:1; Num 18:7). Primarily, the high priest directed the corporate worship of God among the people of God. In order to do that well, he had to maintain holy conduct (Lev 21:6-8). He was responsible for overseeing the entire priestly community (2 Chron 19:11). Oftentimes, the people would seek the high priest to discern the will of God (Num 27:21) and trust in his ability to prophesy correctly (John 11:51).

To prepare Aaron and his family for their worship leading tasks, they had to be anointed. By utilizing the best of resources (Ex 30:22), a sacred anointing oil was to be blended (Ex 30:25) for the purpose of consecrating the priests for this sacred service (Ex 30:30). This type of anointing oil was not meant for the ordinary person. In fact, it was supposed to be kept holy for this purpose in order to consecrate these worship leaders for their holy tasks (Ex 30:32).

Unity qualifies us for ministry.

If the oil was not meant for the average worshiper but designated for the worship leader, then it conferred priestly status. In writing Psalm 133, King David connected the anointing oil to be a symbol of the unconfined unity among these worship leaders. As it poured onto Aaron's head, it flowed onto his beard, and dripped onto his robes (Ps 133:2). This type of unity is a qualifying, all-encompassing, overflowing essential for the worship leader. If the worship leader is supposed to unite people together to point them to the LORD, how could he not be united with those he serves beside?

What about the dew of Hermon? Being the highest mountain peak in the region, Mount Hermon towered over other mountains around it. Being a standard higher than all the rest, the surrounding mountains and areas benefitted from the refreshing dew that would fall from its peak (Ps 133:3). Unity does not expect the tallest mountains to shrink and the smallest mountains to grow. Unity does not mean uniformity but conformity.

Blessings will flow to all when they unite to one thing rather than one another. For when you unite to one thing, you naturally unite to one another. We all begin to sing the same pitch. With one voice, we begin to glorify our Lord (Rom 15:6). We maintain the unity given to us by the Spirit (Eph 4:3), and we are able to stand firm in one spirit with one mind striving side by side for the faith of the gospel (Phil 1:27).

Unity is found not in looking at one another but looking together at one thing.

If you are trying to serve God but cannot serve him alongside others, you've got a dilemma that must be worked out. Unity qualifies us for ministry. Our Father wants his children to get along. Maybe the greatest thing you can do today to display your allegiance to God is by humbling yourself among his servants.

CONCLUSION

And the Lord said: "Because this people draw near with their mouth and honor me with their lips, while their hearts are far from me, and their fear of me is a commandment taught by men" (Isa 29:13).

The reason we should take these five worship team killers so seriously is due to the significant nature concerning what we do when we worship and when we lead others in worship. Our portrayal of who we worship and how we worship will be accepted and repeated by a majority of our congregations. If we don't get this right, our entire congregations are shortchanged by a subordinate version of God and a measly replacement of entertainment for worship.

With so much at stake, how can we not fight against these assassins? Jesus is deserving of worship, and, as leaders, we must war against any tendency in us that could distract from the one who deserves all of our praise and all of our devotion. The worship team killers must be identified, challenged, and murdered within us.

1. The solution to pride is **humility**.
2. The solution to inconsistency is **integrity**.
3. The solution to incapability is **excellence**.
4. The solution to detachment is **availability**.
5. The solution to division is **unity**.

How I wish that a simple book like this could cure all of us from the poisons that contaminate our motives. Since I am fully aware regarding the condition of my own heart, I understand that these killers are never rid from us indefinitely. They keep coming back and often reappear with updated and improved strategies.

I Am the Problem

The reason why each of these killers can render us so helpless is because at the root of each of them is idolatry. We are bent on making worship about us.

1. Since I want to be *noticed*, I struggle with **pride**.
2. Since I want to be *esteemed*, I struggle with **inconsistency**.
3. Since I want to be *lazy*, I struggle with **incapability**.

4. Since I want to be *safe*, I struggle with **detachment**.

5. Since I want to be *right*, I struggle with **division**.

The problem with worship is me, myself, and I. Worship is not a problem because God is insufficient in his gloriousness. I can't blame my idolatrous tendencies on the presence of worship wars in my church while there remain worship wars in my soul.

We may act as if the problem is outside of us, but the problem is inside of us. Even the choices we provide for worship today reveal the sickness. In an attempt to make worship more palatable, churches provide options for every type of worship scenario. We want worshipers to be as comfortable as they possibly can be and fail to realize how that process causes us to isolate ourselves from one another and to lose focus concerning who worship is really supposed to be about. Our churches have worked hard to provide an ecclesiological buffet with the options for each of us to pick and choose what our meals should taste like. Every selection we make for worship has to do with us.

1. **Reverent or Relevant?** Many people disagree with how worship should be designed. While many people want worship to remain solemn and reverential, another group wants worship to feel as if it took a page from the script right out from the world's storyline. What should the feel of worship be?

2. **Casual or Formal?** Regarding clothing, which is more worshipful? Should we be casual and inclusive in our attire or be formal and offer God our "Sunday best?"

Many people struggle with determining if God, who looks at the heart (1 Sam 16:7), is concerned with what we wear. Some people prefer their pastor to wear a tie and others prefer him to wear a t-shirt. It is the same focus on exterior preferences but portrayed simply with a different flavor.

3. **Seeker-Sensitive or Member-Driven?** Is the worship service primarily for the "seeker" that is interested in Christianity but not yet committed? Or is the service supposed to be geared towards the members' preferences? In either scenario, which seeker or member are you talking about? Even within those groups, many different extremes exist.

4. **Traditional or Contemporary?** Many worship purists live by the fact that musical style should no longer change but remain stylistically in an era that they deem sacred or superior. Other people believe that we must speak a musical language that the current culture speaks. Does God have a favorite musical style of worship?

5. **Traditions or Commandments?** The prophet Isaiah chastised the people of God for worrying themselves more with the traditions of man than the commandments of God (Isa 29:13). Jesus would later quote the verse as he addressed the Pharisees obsession with manmade agendas versus God-made truths (Matt 15:8-9; Mark 7:6-7). How much of worship today originates from manmade traditions? When worship wars happen in our churches, are they due to a violation of biblical truth or a compromise of

personal preferences? We make worship about what we want versus what God wants.

6. **Man-Focused or God-Focused?** This choice is the linchpin for all other choices. Is worship about us or God? Worship is not about the seeker or the member. It is not about the senior adult or the emerging generation. Worship is not intended to appease this group or that group. Until we begin to understand that worship is not for us but for God, we will never get it right. Our current practices reveal that we are making worship more about us than we are making it about God (Zech 7:5-6).

What is God's favorite worship style? I can tell you that in heaven, worship wars will no longer exist. We will cease squabbling about what musical style is more God-honoring or man-pleasing. In that moment, we will finally realize what God's favorite worship style really is.

God's favorite worship style is a lifestyle.

The lifestyle of worship blesses the LORD at all times (Ps 33:1) and comes from an overflow of the heart (Matt 12:34). Instead of offering a practical sacrifice, my life is to become the living sacrifice (Rom 12:2). The temple is now portable (1 Tim 3:15; 1 Pet 2:5) as we walk through our lives giving praise to God at every possible moment.

Have you ever wondered why God commands us to worship? Many people question why God would insist on others worshiping him. It sounds self-serving and egotistical. What makes that thought unsubstantiated is the fact that God is not needy. There is nothing that we can offer him that he is dependent upon. Why does God command us to worship? Because it is the best thing for us. Glorifying God with our lives is the best thing for our lives and he is fully aware of that truth. The nearness of God is for our good (Ps 73:28).

It is more important to worship God with our lives than with our lips. Our soul is craving focus and clarity that resonates more than an activity we engage in for just an hour weekly. Worship should be the soundtrack of our lives.

As worship leaders, we must desire the entire package. We fight against pride, inconsistency, inability, detachment, and division because worship is a lifestyle. With the power that God provides us, we strive to lead with humility, integrity, capability, availability, and unity. Why would we work so hard on these issues? Because this standard is what God prescribes in his Word. Worship apart from the Word can never work.

Worship by the Word

During the time of King David, the nation of Israel's arch-nemesis was the Philistine army. In back and forth battles, the Philistines proved to be a constant nuisance for God's people. At one point, they had even stolen the Ark of the Covenant from Israel (1 Sam 5:1). After noticing that the shiny box was always in front of Israel's army when they won the battles, the Philistines thought they could reap the same benefits if they possessed the same equipment as the Israelites.

Unfortunately for the Philistines, possession of the ark did not guarantee victory. After they brought the ark into one of their temples, their idol Dagon was apparently too close to it. One night when no one else was around, it fell face downward and the statue's hands had been cut off (1 Sam 5:4). Apparently, some force of God could have charged with breaking and entering but who was going to arrest him? God was not pleased with non-worshipers handling the things of God. After the Philistines possessed the ark for seven months (1 Sam 6:1), they decided to return this gift that kept on giving unwanted side effects (1 Sam 6:3). Placing it upon a cart (1 Sam 6:8), the Philistines parted ways with the ark and gave it back to the Israelites.

What a day of rejoicing for the Israelites! The Ark of the Covenant, the representation of God's presence, had returned! What did they do as a result? They neglected it. The ark stayed well kept in a closet for seventy-five years. Oh, what tragedy! The presence of God was stuffed in a closet for seventy-five years before someone had enough sense to put the LORD back at his rightful place of centrality among the people.

King David decides to return the ark to Jerusalem but along the way, something shocking took place. The Israelites were transporting the ark on a new cart driven by oxen (2 Sam 6:3). Since the ark was important, they obviously invested in a nice, pristine cart. What was the problem? They learned this practice from the Philistines (1 Sam 6:8).

The people of God learned how to worship God from those who did not know God.

The problem was that God commanded the priests to carry the ark on poles (Ex 25:14). Consecrated leaders were given a consecrated process in order to consecrate the people in order to meet with God. God's work must be done in God's way if it is to have God's blessing. Unfortunately, these Israelites were incorporating worldly practices into holy worship. God's Word was clear on how the worship leaders were to care for the things of the LORD, and they had blatant disregard for the biblical instructions. The leaders decided to do things in a more efficient way and God was not pleased with their innovative rebellion. God's Word made it clear how they were to worship and they abandoned his mandates.

We are called to obey the Word – not imitate the world. You can't worship God if you neglect the Word of God.

During the trip, the assembly is excited. They are going to be able to worship again, but God knows it is dangerous for them to commence worship by their own terms. The subtly of this idolatry was extremely toxic. By appearance, they seemed to care for the things of the LORD but they wanted to experience it according to their own preferences.

God decided to get their attention. When the ox stumbled, the ark teetered on the cart, and a man named Uzzah standing nearby braced it with his hand. Uzzah did what every single one of us would have done if we saw something sacred or valuable about to fall into the dirt – you try to catch it.

How does God reward Uzzah for his sensitivity towards the things of the LORD? God strikes him dead (2 Sam 6:7). Uzzah presumed his hands were cleaner than the dirt. He was dead wrong. As this religious procession commenced, God reminded them that intentions without integrity is insufficient. They had to remember the awesome and yet terrifying presence of the LORD before they went a step further.

It is a dangerous thing to enter into the presence of God and somehow believe that you deserve to be there.

In the middle of this euphoric worship processional, things get real awkward real quick. Jubilation quickly turned into intimidation. As modern believers, you may feel relieved that this story is just an Old Testament example of when God was a little more intense in the wrath department, but you must realize that this account is more than an isolated event. God has always taken worship very seriously. When Nadab and Abihu offered strange fire before the LORD that went against biblical commandments (Lev 10:1), God struck them down to get the attention of the nation (Lev 10:2). God didn't get soft in the New Testament either which is seen through his judgement against attention-seeking Ananias and Sapphira. In an attempt to garner the praise of people in the church with their gift, they sought to deceive the leaders concerning the amount given and God kills them for their disobedience (Acts 5:5, 10).

God takes worship very seriously, and he expects worship leaders to lead the people according to the specific standards expressed in Scripture.

Can you imagine what it was like when Uzzah went down? In the middle of this worship event, one of the worship leaders is struck down dead in front of everyone. Needless to say, David didn't want the ark near him anymore. So what did he do? He instructs a lesser-known priest named Obed-edom, who lives ten miles outside the city, to take the ark into his own home (2 Sam 6:10). The Ark of the Covenant – which had just killed a man for touching it – moved into his living room for three months until King David figured out what to do with it. I know how hard it is to make my children not touch the remote control or the electrical socket, can you imagine trying to convince your children not to put their grimy hands on the big shiny thing in the middle of the living room?

Three months later, David heard that God was blessing Obed-edom, and so he decided it must be safe enough to bring the ark back to Jerusalem, but this time, he would return it while obeying God's instructions. Restarting the processional, David gets consecrated worship leaders to handle the things of God and carry the ark on poles again. Just after traveling six steps, they stop and make an offering just in case someone had sinned in that short distance traveled (2 Sam 6:13).

David brings the ark into the city with much rejoicing and dancing and the presence of God is symbolically back in the center of God's people – where it should have been the entire time. The greatest of leaders was also the most passionate of worshipers. King David stripped himself of royalty in the presence of the King of kings. He became just like every other worshiper.

Can't Settle for Less

When happens next in the narrative should profoundly impact all worship leaders. When the Bible lists out the people in charge of caring for the ark and the temple, Obed-edom's name comes up repeatedly. Obed-edom is listed as a worship leader on the lyre (1 Chron 15:21), a gatekeeper to the ark (1 Chron 16:38), and a minister in the temple (1 Chron 26:4, 12-15).

Don't you wish he was on your volunteer team? The guy is absolutely everywhere! Remember – he lived ten miles away. He couldn't just hop in the minivan throughout the day to get there. The investment it required of him is noteworthy.

Once someone truly experiences the presence of God, he can never settle for less again.

After worshipping the LORD at such a close proximity for three months, Obed-edom was addicted to being near God. He couldn't exist without God's presence. He probably uprooted his family and moved cities so he could be close to the one he loved the most. When the call was made for someone to stand at the entrance of the ark, he signed up. Just to be a doorkeeper in the house of God got him one step closer to the presence of God (Ps 84:10). He would play, sing, or serve in anyway possible just to be close to God. Once you have experienced the presence of God, it is near impossible to continue with anything lesser.

So what about you? When was the last time you truly experienced the presence of God? You worshiped him so close that any deviation from his presence was too much of a calamity to endure. Obed-edom shows us that our proximity to God is directly proportional to our productivity for God. He shows us that no substitute will ever do once we have truly experienced communing with God.

This entire narrative teaches us the importance of worshiping according to the teachings from the Word. In reality, the entire narrative of the Bible is working towards the reconciliation between God and man (2 Cor 5:20). God is turning rebels into worshipers. God is able to teach us (Ps 51:6) and we in turn should teach others (Ps 51:13). From rebels to worshipers, from worshipers to worship leaders, God transforms us but he does it by directing us according to his Word. We are to worship him in spirit and in truth (John 4:23) and not in flesh and in lies.

If we operate from pride, inconsistency, inability, detachment, and division, we are attempting to lead others in worship in direct conflict with the teachings from the Word. If we desire to be used mightily by God in order to point others clearly to God, we will lead according to scriptural mandates. We will lead with humility, integrity, excellence, availability, and unity.

A successful worship leader is one who causes people to forget the one leading and to remember the one to whom they have been led.

Our job is to lead people to encounter Jesus. There is no greater goal than to decrease so that Christ can increase (John 3:30). Clear the path and allow the people to see him for who he truly is (Isa 62:10). Don't let these worship team killers get in the way of the incomparable view of the unrivaled Savior.

Made in the USA
Columbia, SC
03 August 2022